Cleansing the Sanctuary of the Heart:
Tools for Emotional Healing

Cleansing the Sanctuary of the Heart:

Tools for Emotional Healing

David and Beverly Sedlacek

TATE PUBLISHING
AND ENTERPRISES, LLC

Cleansing the Sanctuary of the Heart: Tools for Emotional Healing, Second Edition
Copyright © 2014 by David and Beverly Sedlacek. All rights reserved.

No part of this publication may be reproduced, stored in a retrieval system or transmitted in any way by any means, electronic, mechanical, photocopy, recording or otherwise without the prior permission of the author except as provided by USA copyright law.

Scripture quotations marked "KJV" are taken from the Holy Bible, King James Version, Cambridge, 1769. Used by permission. All rights reserved.

Scripture quotations marked "NKJV" are taken from The New King James Version / Thomas Nelson Publishers, Nashville: Thomas Nelson Publishers. Copyright © 1982. Used by permission. All rights reserved.

Scripture quotations marked "NAS" are taken from the New American Standard Bible ®, Copyright © 1960, 1962, 1963, 1968, 1971, 1972, 1973, 1975, 1977, 1995 by The Lockman Foundation. Used by permission. All rights reserved.

Scripture quotations marked "NIV" are taken from the Holy Bible, New International Version ®, Copyright © 1973, 1978, 1984 by International Bible Society. Used by permission of Zondervan Publishing House. All rights reserved.

Scripture quotations marked "NLT" are taken from the Holy Bible, New Living Translation, Copyright © 1996. Used by permission of Tyndale House Publishers, Inc. All rights reserved.

This book is designed to provide accurate and authoritative information with regard to the subject matter covered. This information is given with the understanding that neither the author nor Tate Publishing, LLC is engaged in rendering legal, professional advice. Since the details of your situation are fact dependent, you should additionally seek the services of a competent professional.

The opinions expressed by the author are not necessarily those of Tate Publishing, LLC.

Published by Tate Publishing & Enterprises, LLC
127 E. Trade Center Terrace | Mustang, Oklahoma 73064 USA
1.888.361.9213 | www.tatepublishing.com

Tate Publishing is committed to excellence in the publishing industry. The company reflects the philosophy established by the founders, based on Psalm 68:11,
"The Lord gave the word and great was the company of those who published it."

Book design copyright © 2014 by Tate Publishing, LLC. All rights reserved.
Cover and interior design by Nathan Harmony

Published in the United States of America
ISBN: 978-1-62902-227-7
1. Christian Living: Psychology
2. Religion: Christianity: Christian Life- Suffering & Grief
14.02.18

Forward to the Second Edition

Time has a way of moving forward, and as we have grown in our personal lives, so have our ideas and experiences in the area of emotional healing. We understand much more about grace than we did six years ago when Cleansing the Sanctuary of the Heart: Tools for Emotional Healing was first written. We have experienced Jesus more deeply and personally for ourselves. Therefore, our continuing journey with our best Friend is reflected in this second edition. We have also learned much about neuroscience that is of tremendous benefit to understanding how our bodies, souls and spirits work together in wondrous harmony. Truly, we are fearfully and wonderfully made. Beverly has been blessed by a study of neuroscience and has included many insights from her study into this edition.

Since the publication of the first edition, we have developed is a *Workbook* that accompanies this book. It has many useful exercises that helps individuals or groups on their journey to cleansing the sanctuary of their hearts.

We have also developed our thinking and practice in the area of forgiveness. This chapter has been updated as well. We have grown from sitting at the feet of others such as Pastor Terry Wardle at Ashland Theological Seminary. His rich insights and vulnerable sharing from his own journey of healing have blessed us immensely and helped to organize our thinking.

We have met many new friends in the past six years and have transitioned from Oakwood University in Huntsville, Alabama to Andrews University in Berrien Springs, Michigan. David currently teaches at the Seventh-day Adventist Theological Seminary. Beverly teaches in the Department of Nursing at Andrews and has a private counseling practice in Berrien Springs. Our prayer is that this edition will be a blessing to those who read it. You bless us when you invest your time and energy to work on emotional healing.

David and Beverly Sedlacek

Acknowledgment

We are indebted to many pioneers in the field of biblical psychology including John and Paula Sandford, Larry Crabb, Dan Allender, Neil Anderson, Sandra Wilson, Oswald Chambers, and Ellen White. Their ideas have been incorporated into this manuscript. We have placed gems from their work into the setting of the sanctuary. We are grateful for the contribution of these pioneers and so many others who prayed for the success of this project.

David and Beverly

Table of Contents

Introduction.. 11

Chapter 1
Biblical Psychology............................. 17

Chapter 2
Cleansing the Sanctuary of the Heart:
Hope in Our Wonderful High Priest.............. 25

Chapter 3
Healing Broken Hearts and Wounded Spirits:
Opening Our Hearts to Jesus.................... 39

Chapter 4
The Law of Love: God's Antidote for Sin 81

Chapter 5
The Height and Depth of Law:
What Was Natural Became Unnatural............. 97

Chapter 6
The Laws of Honor, Judging, Vows, and Faith:
God's Accommodation for Sin.................. 109

Chapter 7
Forgiveness: Love in Action.................... 121

Chapter 8
Repentance for Sin: Cleansing Your Temple 149

Chapter 9
False Beliefs: The Truth Will Make You Free 183

Chapter 10
Death to Self: The Only Way to Life............ 197

Chapter 11
Boundaries in Scripture:
Maintaining the Life within Us 217

Introduction

The sanctuary is about relationships. Its essence is about experiencing God and His covenant love for us, His wounded, fallen creation. As we trace the events that preceded God giving Moses the instructions for building the sanctuary in Exodus 25, we see that God first delivered the children of Israel from the bondage of slavery to the Egyptians. He wanted them to lay hold of their heritage as the children of Abraham. In Exodus 6:2-8, God renewed His everlasting covenant with the children of Israel by telling them, through Moses, that He was the God of Abraham, Isaac, and Jacob with whom He established the covenant. He reassured them that He heard their cry. God remembered His covenant and declared that He would take them as His people and deliver them. However, the children of Israel were not able to grasp this good news "for anguish of spirit and for cruel bondage" (Exodus 25:9, KJV). God wanted to reconnect His people with Himself. However, after four hundred years in bondage, their faith was very weak. Although God drowned Pharaoh's army, the children of Israel struggled to trust God when faced with thirst and hunger. When given the assurance that they could go directly into the Promised Land if they believed that God was strong enough to enable them to conquer the giants who lived there, most of them thought that this good news was too good to be true.

We smugly look at the "hardheartedness" of the Israelites and declare that if only we had been there, things would have been different. If God did all of those miraculous signs for us, surely we would believe. What we fail to realize is that "unbelief" and "disobedience" (see Hebrews 3:19, KJV) are the byproduct of years of bondage, slavery, and abuse. Victims develop a mindset of hopelessness and negative expectation. They cannot see beyond the darkness of the past. God saw that the children of Israel were not yet ready for the Promised Land. They could not yet grasp His love for them, the desired of His heart.

He saw that He would have to teach them about Himself and His ways. Therefore, He gave them the commandments and the statutes to teach them how relationships with Him and with others work best. When the children of Israel presumptuously stated, "All that the Lord hath spoken we will do" (Exodus 19:8, KJV), God saw that they misunderstood the nature of the covenant He established with Abraham. The everlasting covenant was about what God alone could do, and would do, for the people who were the objects of His love. He romanced them by telling them that they were His special people through whom He wanted to do great things so that the nations of the world would experience God's glory. For abused people, it is hard to believe that all they have to do is receive and believe. "The very God of peace sanctify you wholly...faithful is He who calls you who also will do it" (1 Thessalonians 5:23-24, KJV). Experience has taught them that they have to perform to be accepted, that somehow they have to be good enough, or that they must earn love. The children of Israel misunderstood that the commandments were relational instructions about how to love the Lord with all their hearts and their neighbors as themselves.

God saw that they needed a visual representation to help them see that His desire was to be with them, to be intimately connected with each of their lives. Therefore, He gave them the sanctuary service. The sacrifice of innocent lambs on the altar of burnt offering was designed to show them that He loved them so much that He would die for them. The rest of the sanctuary service demonstrated how He would restore them completely into communion with Himself.

To one degree or another, we all have been traumatized by the abuse of "Egyptian" bondage. Rather than entering the Promised Land as soon as God desired, we are in the school of the wilderness learning to trust God. We have marginalized the sanctuary service to a study of furniture and function, and we completely missed what it shows us about God's heart. "Thy way, O Lord, is in the sanctuary" (Psalm 77:13, KJV). Cleansing the sanctuary is for the sole purpose of fallen humanity becoming at one (atonement) with God. It is less about law and sin than it is about the Savior. It is not about the fear of judgment, but rather about the assurance of restoration. It is His way. This work is dedicated to lifting up Jesus, our Great High Priest, and sharing the things we have learned from Him.

Those who have been touched by healing using this new covenant sanctuary experience have encouraged us to share the principles used at Into His Rest Ministries. We want many others to benefit as well. We do not believe that we have all the answers but are learning every day from those we work with. It is our fervent prayer that this work will be a blessing to all who read it. Expect that as you read, the Spirit of God will be working in your heart. You may experience conviction. Some of you may experience the opening of wounds long submerged. Our prayer is that you will also experience the personal healing power of Christ. We pray that in return, you will love Him with all your heart and with all your soul and with all your mind and with all your strength (Mark 12:30, KJV).

The stories of inhumane abuse that we hear from both men and women who are struggling to live the Christian life produce in us heart-wrenching sadness and fierce indignation. Our sadness comes from the fact that human beings can treat one another this way. We will share many of these real stories of pain with you. It is our hope that the courage shown by those we have heard will strengthen you to walk through your "valley of the shadow of death" too. Although we have changed their names, the people we discuss are real. Their pain and their healing are real. Through the personal intervention of a loving heavenly Father, a personal Savior, an ever-present Comforter, and a multitude of ministering angels, we have witnessed miracles.

You may identify with these stories as you read. In this book, many suggestions are given to help readers work through a process of healing. Prayer for divine light may result in fruit being produced in your life as well. Many of us have loved darkness because it has been comfortable. We have been afraid of having our pain exposed to the light of truth. However, just as a seed must be planted in the ground before new life can spring up, so it is with us. First, we must die to self so that new life can emerge. While dying is frightening to the wounded, fear of death leads to continued bondage (see Hebrews 2:15, KJV). We pray that you will find freedom and release from suffering as you continue your journey—with Jesus always at your side.

David and Beverly Sedlacek

Chapter 1
Biblical Psychology

> *"The true principles of psychology are found in the Holy Scriptures. Man does not know his own value. He acts according to his unconverted temperament of character because he does not look unto Jesus, the Author and Finisher of his faith."*
>
> Ellen G. White

"Psychology" is a modern word. In the late nineteenth and twentieth centuries, its practice has, in effect, replaced the community acceptance of God's sovereignty in the lives of human beings, or more specifically, in the life of the human soul and mind. In many contemporary Christian writings, the word has a dissonant sound because psychology has not been a term or practice traditionally considered spiritual or religious. In fact, it has been associated with practitioners and philosophers who are not only humanist in perspective, but also often decidedly atheistic. For who but a human being confident of his own power over himself would presume to study the workings of the human mind and soul, much less be in control of his own?

The word "psychology" literally means the "study of the soul" in Greek. For those of us who consider ourselves religious, the soul is God's domain. Another perspective popular among religious groups, however, is that psychology is actually a study of the workings of evil spirits upon, and in, the human soul and mind. This viewpoint sees the practice of psychology as Satanic, or at least invalid, since it does not include God. Whether a negative view of psychology arises from the practice of twentieth and twenty-first century humanists or from the resistance of religious dogmatists is irrelevant. There has been a misunderstanding of the true purpose and principles of psychology, as they are understood from God's point of view.

Since the word of God is a complete guide for human life, Christians would expect to find principles of psychology in the Bible. Given the above dilemma, however, can there be such a thing as "biblical" psychology? Some Christians suspect that "biblical psychology" is just a form of spiritualism in disguise. Because we as practitioners believe that there are true principles for the healing of the soul and mind to be found in the Scriptures, we have based our practice upon these principles. Unfortunately, efforts to pervert these principles, or to cause even Christians to ignore them, have been understandably successful in this late, anti-religious time in history.

In our own search for truth, we have sought to find principles in the Scriptures that reflect and can be applied to the workings of the human mind and heart. The hurting human heart is less concerned with intellectual abstractions than it is with experiencing relief. Jesus, in fact, spent more time healing than He did preaching or teaching. This was how He introduced people to His ministry and opened their hearts to hear His message of salvation. In Matthew 17:11, Jesus said, "Indeed Elijah is coming first and will restore all things" (NKJV). This reference to John the Baptist, who prepared the way for the first coming of Christ, is connected to the prophecy of Malachi 4:5,6, "Behold, I will send you Elijah the prophet before the coming of the great and dreadful day of the Lord. And he will turn the hearts of the fathers to the children, and the hearts of the children to their fathers" (NKJV). Elijah, who Jesus refers to as John the Baptist (Matthew 17:11-13), was to prepare the way for the coming of the Lord. Today, as we await the second coming of Jesus, we do not look for the literal return of the person of Elijah. Rather, it is the corporate mission of the church to prepare for His coming.

Malachi 4:6 instructs us that the essence of this work of preparation is related to healing hearts. Relationships between parents and children are to be restored. Since the essence of sin is a break in relationship with God and with fellow human beings, the restoration of all things is also relational. Fallen human beings are not capable of this restoration apart from God. It is by an infusion of His perfect love that we can love Him and others. It is our responsibility to depend on Him for the healing of our hearts and for the indwelling of His Spirit. He will not force Himself upon us, even to heal us. We must desire to love Him passionately and purely. If this desire is not in us, God will give it to us if we ask for it. God promises that there will be a group of people living on earth before He comes again in whom the character (the perfect love) of Jesus will have been fully restored. Those who have been courageous enough to pursue a healing experience will be especially well prepared for this ultimate experience of "following the Lamb withersoever He goeth" (Revelation 14:4, KJV).

Because people are hurt by other people, healing usually takes place most effectively with other people and often in a group. God's plan, then, is that He uses other people to work with Him in this ministry of healing. "All praise to the God and Father of our Lord Jesus Christ. He is the source of every mercy and the God who comforts us. He comforts us in all of our troubles so that we can comfort others. When others are troubled, we will be able to give them the same comfort God has given us (2 Cor. 1:3-4, NLT). God's people will have walked through the valley of their own shadow of pain and will bear this burden with others. They will have learned to rejoice in the suffering that has been permitted by God because it has strengthened them to stand when thousands are falling at their side and ten thousand at their right hand.

The Scriptures are the basis and ultimate source for the study of the soul. If the principles of psychology are found in the Holy Scriptures, then Jesus, as the savior of humankind, must have been the psychologist par excellence! Dealing with the minds of people is a great and delicate work, truly the work of God. If this work is the work of God, then there must be a way of doing it that is in perfect harmony with God's word. Rather than being evil, true psychology will make the Gospel real to those to whom we minister. We must draw theological principles from the pages of the word of God and apply them to our lives in order to relieve the pains, perplexities, and weights that we as humans carry.

It is necessary to study "psychology" directly from the Scriptures in order to lead souls to Christ. However, we are not the only ones who have been studying the human mind. Satan has had thousands of years also to study it. He knows it well, and is subtly attempting to fill human minds with his thoughts. In fact, Satan's counterfeits in psychology today are so close to the powerful workings of the Holy Spirit that many seekers are blinded to the Spirit's workings. Fearing entrapment by Satan, they throw out the very means by which the Spirit seeks to free them from Satan's evil snares. Remember that Jesus Himself was accused on many occasions of being a devil.

True biblical psychology turns the hearts of men and women to Christ. Parents stand in God's place, intended by God to represent Him until children grow into the knowledge of God for themselves. Because many parents represent God poorly, their children need to have a clearer picture of God. Christian counselors, when they treat their clients with patience, kindness, and love, are presenting a true picture of God. They help clients dare to believe that God loves them. They come to find the rest, joy, and peace of mind that for so long has eluded them.

They come to love not only with their heads, but also with their hearts.

Most Christians desire to have an intimate union with Jesus Christ. However, their best efforts have not resulted in a relationship with Him that seems real to them. They do not understand the circumstances of their lives. Their prayers seem to go unheard. They are filled with doubt, guilt, and shame. They reach out for God, often time after time, but do not seem to find Him.

As counselors, we have sought to be human conduits who will stand in the gap to connect those in need with their personal Savior. Although they may have been warned against confiding in a human being rather than Christ, they are unable to grasp an unseen God alone. Indeed, the focus of a counseling ministry is to position these hurting ones so they can experience Christ as their healer. Wounded ones need a compassionate, empathic human ear to hear the burden of pain, shame, and guilt that they carry. However, many are often too angry with God or too hurt by others to go directly to Christ for healing and forgiveness. We do not believe that the counselor should "hear confession," so to speak, because Scripture is clear that only God is able to forgive sin (Luke 5:21, KJV). While it is true Christians should pour their hearts out to God, Jesus the Great Shepherd appointed undershepherds (John 21:15-17) to feed the sheep, to have a tender regard for sinners, to treat them with divine compassion, and to listen to their stories of pain, suffering, degradation, and misery. Christian counselors provide a "human ear" that will position those who have been hurt to the ear of Christ and help them believe that, no matter what they have done, they have been heard, healed, and forgiven.

Christian counselors dare not rely on their own wisdom, or on the knowledge or skills that they learned in school. They must be men and women of prayer who have learned to trust God with all of their hearts. They must be on their own journey toward healing and wholeness. Only then are they safe to support others to experience what they themselves have.

We pray that God's light and intelligence will shine forth in and through this work that He may be glorified through a ministry of healing to His saints in these last days.

Chapter 2

Cleansing the Sanctuary of the Heart: Hope in Our Wonderful High Priest

"And let them make me a sanctuary; that I may dwell among them."

(Exodus 25:8, KJV*)*

As we begin this work, we would like to establish a Scriptural framework for the healing process in order to best understand the illumination and beauty that God wants to place within the human heart and mind. He wants to give us nothing less than the fullness of the beauty of His presence. In order to do this, we must have an understanding of the biblical prophecies that apply to spiritual healing.

Jesus is now ministering as our great High Priest in the sanctuary in heaven. This is a fulfillment of the twenty-three-hundred day prophecy of Daniel 8:14: "And he said unto me, unto two thousand and three hundred days; then shall the sanctuary be cleansed" (KJV). Every day of the year in ancient Israel, sinners brought their offerings to the priest to be sacrificed on the altar of burnt offering as an atonement for their sins (Leviticus 1-7). One day a year on the Day of Atonement, the High Priest would enter the Most Holy Place to cleanse the sanctuary or to make atonement for the sins the people committed the previous year (Leviticus 16). These Old Testament sacrifices prefigured events that would occur in the lives of Christ and his people. For example, lambs slain on the altar of burnt offering prefigured, or were a type of, Christ's death on the cross (the antitype). Likewise, the high priest's ministry in the most holy place on the Day of Atonement was a type of Christ's ministry for us today in the heavenly sanctuary. Thus, we can say that we are now living in the antitypical Day of Atonement. This was the day when sin was not only forgiven, but also blotted out of the most holy place of the sanctuary.

If we are living in the antitypical Day of Atonement, then there must be a corresponding work going on today. It is easy to believe that Christ is cleansing sin from the heavenly sanctuary, but what about His work of cleansing the sanctuary of our hearts (1 Cor. 6:19)? According to Scripture, the blotting out of sin in us is more than a possibility. It is both a promise and the assurance of the good news of the Gospel: "Now may the God of peace Himself sanctify you entirely; and may your spirit and soul and body be preserved complete, without blame at the coming of our Lord Jesus Christ. Faithful is He who calls you, and He also will bring it to pass" (1 Thessalonians 5:23-24,

NASB). Victorious living is promised numerous places in Scripture (e.g., Jude 24; 1 Cor. 10:13; 1 Peter 1:4-10). It is equally clear from these Scriptures that such victorious living is done by faith in the power of God, not in the efforts of frail humans alone.

The purpose of this book is to give the church God's tools "that He might sanctify and cleanse it with the washing of water by the word, that He might present it to Himself a glorious church, not having spot, or wrinkle, or an such thing; but that it should be holy and without blemish (Ephesians 5:26-27, KJV).

It is hard for those who have been wounded to comprehend the sublime possibilities of having no spot or wrinkle. They have settled for the life of the downtrodden. They feel anything but "pure and holy." Wounded ones feel the reality of Isaiah 1:5-6: "The whole head is sick and the whole heart is faint. From the sole of the foot even unto the head there is no soundness in it; but wounds and bruises, and putrefying sores: they have not been bound up, neither mollified with ointment" (KJV). When they allow themselves to feel, they feel fractured and anything but complete. They experience themselves as defiled and damaged to the core.

However, it is our conviction that wounded ones who have been healed and who have overcome sin will be better prepared to endure the trials ahead than those who have not been severely tested. Their deepest hurts will be transformed into bastions of strength. "Strengthen ye the weak hands, and confirm the feeble knees. Say to them that are of a fearful heart, be strong, fear not: behold your

God will come with a vengeance, even God with a recompense: he will come and save you" (Isaiah 35:3-4, KJV). "The Lord builds up Jerusalem: he gathers the outcasts of Israel. He heals the brokenhearted and binds up their wounds" (Psalm 147:2-3, NASB). We declare the truth to those who have been deeply hurt: no matter how things appear, Jesus is at work on your behalf in the sanctuary above and in your heart here on earth. Be encouraged as the groundwork for God's plan of healing and sanctification is laid.

When we look at ourselves, the rest and peace that are promised as a result of overcoming may appear to be an impossibility. Wounded ones easily despair of attaining to this high and holy calling (Philippians 3:14, KJV). They have tried so hard to do right, hoping that by doing so they might be at peace. Almost in despair, we ask, *How can we reach the perfection described by our Lord and Savior Jesus Christ—our great Teacher? Can we meet His requirement and attain to so lofty a standard?* We can, or else Christ would not have asked us to do so. He is our righteousness. In His humanity, He has gone before us and wrought out perfection of character. We are to have the faith in Him that works by love and purifies the soul. Perfection of character is based upon our relationship to Christ. If we are constantly dependent upon the merits of our Savior, and walk in His footsteps, we shall be like Him, pure and undefiled. He would not ask of us anything that He is not able to give us the grace and strength to do. "For nothing is impossible with God" (Luke 1:37, NLT). "If you sinful people know how to give good gifts to your children, how much more will your heavenly Father give good gifts to those who ask him" (Matthew 7:11, NLT).

Though we may know that by faith we "are complete in Him" (Colossians 2:10, KJV), we ask, *How does the Lord work out the process of perfecting His character in us?* Answers are again found in a study of the sanctuary service. In 1 Corinthians 6:19, we read the following: "Or do you not know that your body is the temple of the Holy Spirit who is in you...?" (NASB). Is there an analogy between the temple in heaven and our bodies as the temple of the Holy Ghost? We believe that there is a clear parallel.

We are the Temple

"Or do you not know that your body is the temple of the Holy Spirit *who is* in you, whom you have from God, and you are not your own?" (1 Cor. 6:19, NKJV).

"And the very God of peace sanctify you wholly: and I pray God your whole spirit and soul and body be preserved blameless unto the coming of our Lord Jesus Christ" (1 Thess. 5:23, KJV).

As temples of the indwelling Spirit, human beings are composed of a spirit, soul, and body. There is an interesting analogy, imperfect though it may be, with the structure of the temple given by God. In the structure of the sanctuary, there was an outer court, a framework or protection for the actual temple itself. The body serves this purpose for our "inner man" and, therefore, may be considered the "outer court" of man. The temple itself was divided into two compartments: the holy place and the most holy place. The holy place had three articles within it: the table for the Bread of the Presence, the lamp stand, and the altar of incense (Exodus 25 and 30). Every day, the priest would bring blood from the sacrifices offered into the holy place and sprinkle it on the curtain, separating the holy place from the most holy place. The purpose of the daily round of ceremonies in the holy place was for the forgiveness of known, confessed sin. We perform a holy place function when sin is recalled and sincerely confessed. If we are the temple or dwelling place of God, what part of us most closely relates to the holy place compartment of the temple? The soul, that part of us that has conscious awareness, memory, and the ability to choose, seems to fit best with the holy place function. At creation, according to Genesis 2:7, "the Lord God formed man of the dust of the ground, and breathed into his nostrils the breath of life; and man became a living soul" (NKJV). The New International Version calls the soul "a living being." The New Living Translation uses the phrase "a living person." The conscious functions of a living soul, being, or person include the will, the ability to plan and create, the awareness of life and surroundings, the emotions, and the memory. They can be considered holy place functions.

There are also aspects of the mind that are less open to scrutiny: the heart and its motives, repressed thoughts, memories, and feelings that have been too painful to acknowledge. To explore these aspects of the mind, we turn to a discussion of the most holy place. As God dwelt in the most holy place of the earthly temple, manifesting His presence by the Shekinah glory, so He wants to dwell in man. What then is the counterpart to the most holy place in us? There appear to be two parallel, interrelated applications. The first is that the most holy place of man is the spirit. A basic understanding of the concept of the spirit is that it is the character. God's Spirit indwelling and thus sanctifying our characters will give us the experience of "Christ in you, the hope of glory" (Colossians 1:27, KJV). This experience of His glory in us is the antitype of His presence in the Shekinah glory. Since the essence of the character of God is that He is love, when His love fills us, His indwelling love is the antidote for sin in the human heart, the dwelling place of God. We will address the idea of the spirit of man more fully in the next chapter.

Another perspective of the most holy place is that it represents the heart or mind, which is considered the seat of the emotions, affections and motives, many of which are unknown or unconscious to us. Scripture refers to the heart. "The heart is deceitful above all things and desperately wicked: who can know it?" (Jeremiah 17:9, KJV). For purposes of our discussion the mind and heart are used interchangeably based on discoveries in neuroscience. Neuroscience deals with the brain's physical structures and physiology. This relatively new scientific branch has opened up exciting understandings of how the mind is ultimately a dynamic aspect of the brain that can be influenced by relationships. Likewise, the brain and its development shape and influence those very same relationships.[2]

Is the idea of an "unconscious" a biblical concept? Scripture does contain the idea of living with undivided hearts and minds. In fact, findings in neuroscience help in our understanding of just how the division occurs. The human brain is made up of a left and right hemisphere. While both sides of the brain are involved in just about every activity, the two hemispheres function differently. The right hemisphere develops even in the womb and processes in a more intuitive and holistic way. One important function of the right brain is to interpret all the non-verbal signals received from mothers. This is an important function, especially for growing infants because between 60-90 percent of all communication between humans is nonverbal. Long before they can speak, babies are taking in and encoding in their neurons all that is going on around them.[3]

The left hemisphere of the brain processes in a logical and sequential manner. It disregards the right-brain emotional elements of trust that are necessary for us to thrive in life.[4] The two hemispheres function best however when they are integrated. Dr. Daniel Siegel, a well-known psychiatrist has written extensively about how recent discoveries in neuroscience and attachment were helping people to change, not only their experiences but also their brains. Using the language of neuroscience, Dr. Siegel labeled the change "increased integration." [5] We see this integration as a point in which the unconscious or heart and mind meet and are fully working together-the left and right brain in balance. In order for this to occur, we must learn to pay attention to right brain experiences- feelings and emotions. We must become aware of what we are feeling and why.

When we fail to pay attention to what we feel and why, we are ignoring feelings and emotions and live with a divided heart, or a "dis-integrated" mind. Coined by Dr. Curt Thompson, a "dis-integrated" mind is the opposite of integration-particularly between various parts of the brain. [6] With a "dis-integrated" mind, we still express unaddressed feelings and emotions, only often in a manner that are harmful to relationships with others.

Consider the following scriptures: "I, the Lord, search the heart, I try the reins, even to give every man according to his ways" (Jeremiah 17:10, KJV). "I am He which searcheth the reins and hearts" (Revelation 2:23, KJV). Some lexicons identify the word "reins" in the literal sense as the kidneys. Figuratively, the reins are our innermost parts, the seat of emotion, affection, and motives—in other words, the heart or secret place of man. Also, consider Psalm 51:6, "Surely you desire truth in the inner parts; you teach me wisdom in the inmost place" (NIV). It is in the inner parts or the inmost place of man that God wants to teach His children truth. This does not refer to doctrinal truth but to truth about themselves, their character flaws, and their brokenness. God also wants to teach His children the truth about His passionate love for them, His trustworthy, patient, and accepting character. This occurs through experience and how we experience God is through our "right brain." When what we know left brain about God and experience him through our feelings and emotions line up, then we experience integration.

Satan has done a masterful job of distorting the image of God to that of a God that should be feared and one whose love is dependent upon performance. We often sing "Tis so Sweet to Trust in Jesus," but the reality for most of us is that there are parts of our hearts and minds that we do not trust Jesus with. Our experience tells us that neither our parents nor God protected us at times in our lives. There are unconscious blocks preventing us from doing what we want to do (See Romans 7). God wants these areas to be brought to light so that He can heal us there. Chapter Three will explain this in more depth.

Unknown sin inhabits large areas of many hearts. When wounded, children prior to conversion respond from the context of the fallen human nature they possess. There is an axiom in recovery that states, "Hurt people hurt people." Hebrews 12:15 describes it this way: "lest any root of bitterness springing up cause trouble, and by this many be defiled" (NKJV). Addressing this point, A. T. Jones wrote that the Lord will probe and bring up "sins to us that we never thought of before, that only shows that he is going down to the depths, and he will reach the bottom at last… He cannot put the seal, the impress of His perfect character, on us until He sees it there. And so He has got to dig down to the deep places we never dreamed of, because we cannot understand our hearts."[5] It is good news that God will reach the bottom of the sin problem in us. It is His commitment to us. "For I am confident of this very thing, that He who began a good work in you will perfect it until the day of Jesus Christ" (Philippians 1:6, NASB).

In Matthew 3:10, John the Baptist said: "And now also the axe is laid unto the root of the trees" (KJV). This analogy from nature describes the work that God wants to do in our hearts. The roots of a plant are below the surface.

We do not see them. For many of us, dealing with the sin problem has been much like pulling up weeds in a garden. We find ourselves sinning and repenting, sinning and repenting, but never having victory over sin. We get frustrated over our lack of victory and conclude that victory is not possible, or we doubt that God is hearing us and answering our prayers. Some are in bitter bondage to self-destructive addictions and mental illnesses. Marital discord and parent/child conflicts deprive others of peace. The roots of all these problems are below the surface, hidden and waiting to be revealed. "For nothing is hidden that will not become evident, nor anything secret that will not be known and come to light" (Luke 8:17, kjv). When we confess a known sin without going to the root below the surface, it is like pulling out a weed in a garden. God has heard our prayer. The sin has been forgiven. The garden looks pretty with all the weeds gone, but shortly the weeds reappear because the roots below the surface have not been destroyed. God promises to search the heart and the mind at all levels (Psalm 139:23-24).

The Scriptures describing God's searching eye may sound threatening. However, these verses are beautiful promises that can be fulfilled in the lives of all who sincerely ask God to open the secret places to them: "Behold, you desire truth in the innermost being, and in the hidden part You will make me know wisdom" (Psalm 51:6, nasb). The blotting out of sin results in the restoration, re-beautification, and reconstruction of human nature. "As we know Jesus better, His divine power gives us everything we need for living a godly life. He has called us to receive His own glory and goodness! And by that same mighty power, He has given us all of his rich and wonderful promises. He has promised that you will escape the decadence all around you caused by evil desires and that you will share in His divine nature" (2 Peter 3-4, NLT). God's promise also is: "A new heart will I give you; and a new spirit will I put within you: and I will take away the stony heart out of your flesh, and I will give you a heart of flesh. And I will put my spirit within you, and cause you to walk in my statutes, and ye shall keep my judgments, and do them" (Ezekiel 36: 26-27, KJV).

A Counterfeit Plan

Satan, an astute Bible student, knows about the blotting out of sin from the most holy place of our hearts. As always, he is ready with a counterfeit. One great evil of modern psychology is the belief that men can heal the minds of other men without the power of God. Secular humanism believes that God is not necessary. One problem with secular humanism in psychology is that God does not get the glory for the healing. Another is that the myth of human self-sufficiency is perpetuated. A third is the danger of putting oneself under the control of another human being. While the predominant approach today in psychology, social work, and counseling is empowerment of the client (the opposite of therapist control), there are still techniques such as hypnosis that give control to another. Wisdom would dictate great caution in using these approaches. Many therapists, whether Christian or not, are very kind, loving, and accepting people. In this, they reflect the character of God even if they do not consciously intend to. Research shows that regardless of the technique or theory used by a therapist, if the client perceives that the therapist cares, there will be improvement. It is good to bear in mind that God starts where people are at. We have worked with many clients whose psychiatrist or therapist saved their lives until they could get access to a Christian counselor. It would appear to be wise, then, to balance a vigilance to recognize the dangers spread before us with the knowledge that "where sin abounded, grace did much more abound" (Romans 5:20, KJV).

However, God is truly the "Divine Psychiatrist," and He uses His Church to minister to others. "And Jesus went about all the cities and villages, teaching in their synagogues, and preaching the gospel of the kingdom, and healing every sickness and every disease among the people. And when he had called unto him his twelve disciples, he gave them power against unclean spirits, to cast them out, and to heal all manner of sickness and all manner of disease" (Matthew 9:35-10:1, KJV). The Church is to be a hospital where the broken, downtrodden, and outcast can come to receive acceptance, love, and help. It is to be a safe place for people to share their grief, sorrow, and struggle with others. The reality is that many church families are still not safe. No effort has been made to provide Christian counseling services for members or for the community. When a person shares sensitive information from the heart, they are often judged and talked about. Some are even thrown out of the church family. This approach is not of God. He ate with publicans, sinners, and prostitutes. God still wants his people to participate in the work of cleansing the sanctuary of the heart, their own first, and then in ministry to others. He wants to use men and women as His conduits to touch the lives of others in a healing ministry. "And all things are from God, who reconciled us to Himself through Christ, and gave us the ministry of reconciliation, namely, that God was in Christ, reconciling the world to Himself, not counting their trespasses against them; and He has committed to us the word of reconciliation. Therefore, we are ambassadors for Christ, as though God were making an appeal through us: we beg you on behalf of Christ, be reconciled to God" (2 Corinthians 5:18-20, NASB).

Today, as at no other time, a healing ministry for the mind is needed. Many secular modalities have been developed. More people are seeking counseling today than ever before, a commentary on the times. It is not too late to learn that God's program works and that the Lord blesses any attempt to heal and be healed His way.

Chapter 3

Healing Broken Hearts and Wounded Spirits:
Opening Our Hearts to Jesus

"He heals the brokenhearted and binds up their wounds"

(Psalm 147:3, NIV*).*

God's healing is all-encompassing. There is no part of the human being that cannot be touched by His divine hand. In the gospels, we learn of His capacity to heal in the physical realm. We remember the case of the paralytic who was let down through the roof by his friends. Jesus said to him, "Son, thy sins be forgiven thee" (Mark 2:5, KJV). Here is an instance in which a *soul* is healed: the paralytic's guilt was removed. He would have known the Lord's blessing even if he had not been physically healed. It is less clearly understood how spirits that have been broken or wounded can be healed; yet this is the most important aspect of healing because it is in our hearts that God seeks to dwell and in our characters that He is to be reflected. In order to examine the subject of healing broken hearts and wounded spirits, we must first define the terms and the context in which they are being used.[1]

Let us first attempt to understand what is meant by the word "spirit." Scripture declares that God breathed "the breath of life" into man's nostrils (Genesis 2:7, KJV). What did God impart to man in His breath? Two elements can readily be identified. The first is "life force" or "vital force." Every human being is given a certain amount of vital force at conception. However, the supply of this life force given at conception is not inexhaustible. Like the energy in a battery, life force can be drawn upon over and over again, but through overwork, poor health habits, addiction, or disease, the life force can be exhausted, resulting in death. In this context, the concept of "life force" is equated with the spirit, which returns to God at the time of death: "…the spirit shall return unto God who gave it" (Ecclesiastes 12:7b, KJV).

In addition to the physical abuse of the body, can the trauma resulting from physical, emotional, verbal, and sexual abuse weaken or diminish this life force? This chapter will explain how abuse in any form profoundly compromises our capacity to live to the fullness originally intended by God.

The first element of the spirit of man, then, is life force; the second is character. John 4:24 says that God is a spirit. Since we are created in the image of God (Genesis 1:26), we must conclude that we also have a spirit similar to God's. Before sin, Adam reflected God's image perfectly. There was no sin or inclination to sin in him. In perfect harmony with God's will, obedience was natural. God's will and man's will were as one. He was physically, mentally, and spiritually like his Maker, the crowning act of His creation. God's plan was to repopulate heaven with man and to use man to assist Him in dealing with the sin problem already present in the universe. Prior to sin, man loved perfectly and did relationships without flaw. What a place Eden must have been! God's plan for man has not changed. Before Jesus comes again, man will again stand in his place with Jesus, the second Adam, leading the way. Humans will again love purely and passionately, will be united with God in every aspect, and will stand against sin that God might eradicate it from the universe. This is the ultimate aim of the work of cleansing the sanctuary of the heart: the restoration of the character of God in the human race. At death, the spirit as character returns to God to be judged by Him in order to see how it reflects His image. "Then the dust will return to the earth as it was, and the spirit will return to God who gave it" (Eccl 12:7, NKJV). God wants to dwell in us fully by the power of the Spirit. Satan's objective is to ruin our character, our spirit, by making us like him.

"For what man knoweth the things of a man, save the spirit of a man which is in him? even so the things of God knoweth no man, but the Spirit of God" (1 Corinthians 2:11, KJV). Our spirit is as real an entity as God, who is Spirit, and the angels, who are ministering spirits. The Scriptures identify several functions that the spirit of man performs. Without the spirit, we would die. The most important function of the spirit, then, is to sustain life. The other functions of the spirit are equally as important. A joyful spirit sustains our health and protects us from disease: "A merry heart doeth good like a medicine: but a broken spirit drieth the bones" (Proverbs 17:22, KJV). This statement is a precise description of what happens physiologically when there has been a breaking of the human spirit through abuse. When a person's spirit is broken, the bone marrow's capacity to produce bone marrow is diminished. A 1998 study by Diane Pappas, MD, JD reveals that emotional abuse is a factor in the depletion of the production of red blood cells.[2] The Bible clarifies that "the life of the flesh is in the blood" (Leviticus 17:11, KJV). The blood is produced in the marrow of the bones.

Have you ever observed the behavior of an abused animal? Adam Katz, a professional dog trainer, on his website defines an abused dog as "any dog that shows specific signs of extreme timidity in response to regular behavior by you." He also reports that abused dogs are confused and engage in fleeing, fighting, or freezing behavior. It is the same with abused people. Repeatedly, we have worked with people who have not only been mentally depressed but physically ill due to a brokenness of spirit. One woman was sexually abused by her brother from the age of three until the age of thirty. As a result, she developed a death wish. After several unsuccessful suicide attempts, she decided that she would kill herself slowly by overeating. Shortly thereafter, she developed lupus, an autoimmune disease by which the body gradually destroys itself. Her death wish was manifested physically.

"The spirit of a man will sustain his infirmity; but a wounded spirit who can bear?" (Proverbs 18:14, KJV). When a person's spirit is vivacious and strong, he will recover from an illness as quickly as his body permits. Recovery from disease is much slower for someone with a broken spirit. Sometimes, the spiritual wounding coupled with the physical illness is even more damaging, and the person dies when he might otherwise have lived.

For many years, the intimate relationship between the mind and body has been studied and affirmed.[3] Whatever affects the body also affects the mind and vice-versa. Much of what is written about the body, mind, and spirit connection tends to be New Age in orientation. However, there are authors such as psychiatrist Gerald May who have written excellent books that include the spirit of man in this mutual interconnectedness.[4] This intimate relationship does not go unnoted in the bible. "A merry heart maketh a cheerful countenance: but by sorrow of the heart the spirit is broken" (Proverbs 15:13, KJV). The grieving process that we go through after the death of a loved one is well understood. Not infrequently, an older spouse's death is quickly followed by the death of the surviving spouse. This is an example of grief that breaks the spirit. The same can be true for infants and children who experience traumatic rejection, abandonment, or loss. Loss of a parent through divorce, death, or emotional absence is a source of deep sorrow. When children are forced to assume adult responsibility too soon, their childhood is lost. When incest occurs, innocence is lost. These significant losses can result in an inability to thrive; rather, there often is a resigned, fatalistic acceptance of the need to survive.

Another important function of the spirit is worship, both corporate and personal. "But the hour cometh and now is when true worshipers shall worship the Father in spirit and in truth" (John 4:23, KJV). Persons with wounded spirits have difficulty rejoicing as Mary did when she met Elizabeth: "My soul doth magnify the Lord, and my spirit hath rejoiced in God my Savior" (Luke 1:46-47, KJV). Their prayers seem to ascend to the ceiling, but no higher. They have difficulty participating wholeheartedly in corporate worship. Since they are not free to "be," they have difficulty connecting with the Source of their being.

Communication is a related function of the spirit. "The Spirit itself beareth witness with our spirit, that we are the children of God" (Romans 8:16, KJV). The Spirit lets us know of our standing with God. In our communication with one another, there is also a spirit-to-spirit factor. We have the ability to sense danger. Many wounded ones have a particularly keen sense of who is safe for them and who is not, based on their need to self-protect.

On the other hand, many who have been broken are very naive and gullible. Because their spirit is crushed, they are not capable of healthy discernment. They get into relationships that hurt them repeatedly. Along this same line, people with wounded spirits have difficulty hearing the voice of their own conscience warning them about sin *in advance*. Only after the fact do they recognize their mistake. The Holy Spirit was at work, but they were not able to hear His voice.

God intends sexual relations to be more than a physical act. In addition to a union of bodies, He intended physical relations to be a spiritual union between husband and wife. "Know ye not that he which is joined to an harlot is one body? For two, saith he, shall be one flesh. But he that is joined unto the Lord is one spirit" (1 Corinthians 6:16, 17, KJV). It is important to understand that a spiritual bond is formed between sexual partners. Most intimate communication is spiritual, a communication between two persons. Sexual relations, for instance, is meant to be a mutual nurturing between two human beings, male and female, who have entered into a covenant relationship with one another. The desire to touch one another at the most intimate level of self, that is, with their physical bodies and their spiritual selves, is both creative and sustaining in nature (see 1 Corinthians 6:19-20).

Spiritual connectedness between human beings often results in human beings "knowing" what the other needs or is thinking without that other person saying a word. If the highest form of communication between humans is spiritual, think how much greater our communication with God is at this level. Scripture says that our spirits pray (1 Corinthians 14:14 KJV). This type of prayer is not dependent upon our mouths. It is the overflowing of a heart that is in love with God. When we are "in love," our spirits sing. "My soul doth magnify the Lord, and my spirit hath rejoiced in God my Savior" was Mary's song of thanksgiving recorded in the first chapter of Luke. Most of us have experienced the rejoicing of spirit when we have been "in love" with a human being. How many of us have had these feelings toward God?

As we have seen, the thoughts and feelings make up the character, or spirit. The sanctified feelings of the spirit are pure: joy, pain, sorrow, etc. Jesus felt pain at this level. He put up no defenses to feeling pain as a human being. We defend against pain by stuffing feelings, suppressing, or repressing the memories of hurtful events because the pain is just too great. We keep ourselves at a distance from those who have hurt us to keep from getting hurt again, but Jesus did not do this. In His spirit (not the Holy Spirit), He felt pure pain, joy, sorrow, and so forth. We also are called upon to experience painful feelings because in doing so, we find healing for ourselves, and the ability to connect with others in their pain (2 Cor. 1:3-4).

A useful distinction can be made between feelings and emotions. Feelings such as pain, rejection, abandonment, and betrayal are primary feelings. They just are. They are felt when a person is hurt. Secondary feelings, or emotions, are reactions to primary feelings when they have not been affirmed, felt, and resolved. For example, many people react to hurt by getting angry. The emotion of anger here is real and powerful, but what is really going on is that the person feels hurt, embarrassed, rejected, or some other primary feeling and cannot express it. In ministering to the spirits of broken people, it is important that they are helped to permit themselves to feel when they have previously believed that it is not okay to feel.

Righteous indignation is a function of the spirit. It is as much an act of love as Jesus' anger was when He cast the moneychangers out of the temple because of His zeal for His Father's house. His were pure and holy feelings. His self-interest was not at all involved. Our emotional reactions, whether they are anger, depression, or fear, are secondary reactions to primary feelings. In most emotional reactions, self comes into play. For example, when people are angry, it is usually because they are not getting their way or they are getting revenge on someone who hurt them. When a person feels self-pity, he or she is self-focused. In our counseling work, we help our clients get to their primary feelings, because healing and forgiveness operate at this level.

Our spirit is necessary to sustain life. If our spirit were to leave our bodies, we would cease to exist. "And He bowed His head and gave up His spirit" (John 19:30, KJV). As we have seen, our spirit comes from God and returns to Him. Our spirit can be wounded. "The spirit of a man will sustain his infirmity; but a wounded spirit who can bear?" (Proverbs 18:14, KJV). Further, it can be broken. "A merry heart doeth good like a medicine: but a broken spirit drieth the bones" (Proverbs 17:22, KJV). These scriptures say that a person with a wounded spirit has trouble maintaining health or overcoming sickness. Sorrow of the heart breaks the spirit. The heart sorrow of wounded children, the loss of loved ones, and oppression can break or wound a person's spirit. Such a spirit has a diminished capacity to sustain life at an optimum level. Life for this person is like a flickering candle (See Proverbs 20:27) that dims in an oxygen-starved environment. Many people suffering from depression have broken spirits. Those who run rather than fight when faced with emotional conflict are often labeled as "cowards." However, we find that these people are often severely wounded ones who do what they must to survive.

We were created to thrive, not merely survive. In fact, God wants us to be conquerors, a far cry from mere survival. Jesus' promise of healing is for those with broken or wounded spirits. The Bible calls the eye the lamp of the body (Matthew 6:22). By looking at someone's eyes, you can tell a great deal about their history of trauma. If there is little sparkle or life in the eye, it may mean that the person has been wounded. Some of the behaviors in American culture that reveal that a person has been wounded include: not being able to look another person in the face (in some cultures); walking with the head hanging down and shoulders stooped; and constant, unnecessary apologies. Scripture says: "Wherefore, lift up the hands which hang down, and the feeble knees" (Hebrews 12:12, KJV). Broken ones need much support in their healing. Often, this support must take human form because these people are not able to lay hold of the "Unseen" alone.

Ultimately, the spirit is meant to be the dwelling place of God. It is the "Most Holy Place" of our temple. The most intimate experience that a human being can have is when God fully possesses His "house" *in them*. In this experience, the human character reflects the character of Christ. As we are "strengthened with might by His Spirit in the inner man" (Ephesians 3:16, KJV), we grow daily into His likeness. To be a fit dwelling place for the God whom they love is the strongest heart cry of every believer. The gospel is a practical teacher of these abstract spiritual disciplines.

At this point, we will discuss the origins of wounding from an experiential view, in order to help us reason from cause to effect. Since we exist in relationship to others, we will attempt to describe the cycle of wounding that occurs in dysfunctional relationships.

The Cycle of Dysfunction

The family has always been God's appointed institution for perfecting the characters of its members. It is the vehicle through which God intends that we prepare to go to heaven. It is in the family we can experience "a little bit of heaven" right here on earth. By his attacks on this divine institution, Satan has been successful in creating dysfunction in many families. Family dysfunction began after sin entered in the Garden of Eden when there was a failure in relationship between man and his wife. Wounding and loss occurs when parents fail to meet basic needs in a child. Dysfunction is seen when ungodly behaviors and responses are manifested in attempts to fill these unmet needs. These choices are sinful because they originate from desires for fulfillment based on human effort and not from God (When my father and mother forsake me, then the Lord will pick me up. Psalm 27.) Dysfunction is passed down from generation to generation. Let's look at addiction to illustrate the cycle of dysfunction.

It must be noted that there can be many causes of family dysfunction including mental illness, prolonged physical illness or disability, poverty, social injustice, and war, to name a few. Addiction is a device that the enemy uses most skillfully to destroy families. In families where addiction is active, there is a disruption of the harmony that God intended. Broadly speaking, addiction is a term encompassing the use of any substance, behavior, emotional state, or relationship by which the marital covenant is broken (physically or spiritually), the sacred family bonds are destroyed, or other relationships are damaged. [5] As much as we would like to believe otherwise, Christians are not exempt from addictions. We bring the dysfunction of our past into our religious experience and into our church family. The reality of the Scripture, "old things have passed away, behold, all things have become new" (2 Corinthians 5:17b, KJV), somehow eludes us. After years of working in the field of addiction, Gerald May, in his classic, *Addiction and Grace*, wrote, "I also learned that all people are addicts, and that addictions to alcohol and drugs are simply more obvious and tragic addictions than others. To be alive is to be addicted, and to be alive and addicted is to stand in need of grace."[6]

This section describes the cycle of dysfunction in which Christians are often trapped and shows God's program to provide healing and bring freedom from bondage. Families can be, and are being, healed and restored to that high and holy standard to which they have been called as they allow God to show them their incredible need.

When we seek a mate, we often enter that relationship with preconceived ideas about how that relationship should be developed or structured. We can readily agree that a functional relationship must have basic characteristics that include love, honesty, communication, trust, loyalty, and friendship. While this list is not all-inclusive, it is extensive enough to see that there are certain basic ingredients essential to the success of an intimate relationship. We can readily agree that these ingredients must be mutual, flowing to and from both parties in a symbiotic nurturing and building process.

Diagram 1

Qualities Desired in A Relationship

Honest

Loyal

Good Communicator

Spiritual

Hard Worker

Good Listener

Sense of Humor

Etc.

Addictions radically alter the sacred give and take of an intimate relationship, whether that relationship is a friendship, a marriage, or a parent/child relationship. Addictions have many faces: work, alcohol, sex, food, religion, drugs, emotions, people and a host of others.

In Diagram Two below, the interference of an addiction in a relationship is illustrated by the letter "A". For the sake of this illustration, we will identify the husband as the one who is caught up in an addiction. As the addiction develops, the relationship begins to suffer. The husband's time and energy are spent in pursuit of the addiction instead of his relationship with his wife and family. The wife finds herself receiving less time and attention. As she begins to experience this change in the relationship, the wife will do what she can to restore the relationship to its previous state of mutuality. Her fear of loss of the relationship leads her to focus more of her time and attention on her husband, in a futile attempt to win him back. Unfortunately, his addictive relationship has superseded his relationship with her, even in its intimacy. His addiction has become, in effect, "the other woman," and the wife finds herself continually losing in the competition for attention. She also finds herself actually becoming addicted to the addict.

Diagram 2

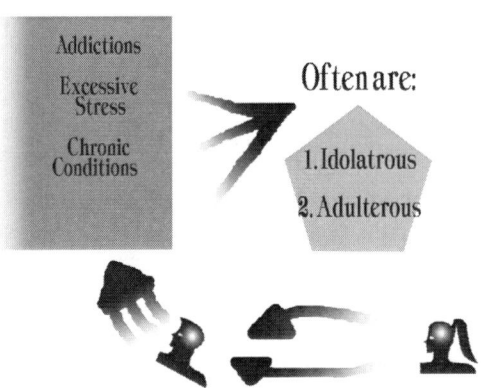

Children born into families where addiction is present are negatively affected by the parents' preoccupation with their illness. Most studies of the emotional needs of children develop lists of various lengths. We believe that these emotional needs are best described as love needs since each of them is an aspect of love. God is love, and parents are designed by God to stand in His place to meet the love needs of their children. The following is a descriptive list of seven basic love needs into which most others fall.

1. <u>Affection</u> It is the responsibility of parents to give plenty of safe, nurturing affection in the form of warm, gentle touch, hugs, and kisses. This develops basic trust, the foundation of character development. Without this, children learn that they must take on a "role" in the family to get their needs met.

2. <u>Affirmation</u> It is important to build a child's sense of worth and capability. A child's sense of both personal and corporate value flows from an adequate number of positive affirmations. Without affirmation, the child develops a deep core of shame about his person. He concludes that he is not important, and this false belief shapes many of his future life choices. Even Jesus was affirmed when His father said, "This is my beloved Son in whom I am well pleased." Encouraging a child gives them a sense that they can do well. Acknowledging their strengths lets them know that they can believe in themselves.

3. <u>Attention</u> In our busy world, it can be difficult to spend an adequate amount of time with our children, but it is worth the investment. Children thrive when they experience parents participating in their lives by attending their school or after school activities, games, and graduations. With plenty of time and attention, children receive a sense that they are important and belong in the family. Spending time with each child alone is important. Do not compare a child with other children. It will give the child either a sense of inferiority or superiority. Acknowledging their achievements reinforces their sense of competence. Many children are forced to become adults too soon by having them always do the things we as adults like to do or by forcing them to assume adult responsibilities before they are developmentally ready. In addictive families, children receive very little positive attention at all. In these families, because attention is meted out when a crisis arises, it often turns out to be negative attention, shown only after a child has acted out. These children often reject their

parents' values simply because the parents showed by their behavior that the child was not valued enough.

4. Protection is more than locks on the doors and instruction not to run out into the street. It is the development and enforcement of family rules designed to give order to the functioning of the family. Without this, children conclude that they must take care of themselves. Protection provides a sense of safety for children, a sense that life is under control, and that they are in control of their world. Children also need emotional protection. They need to know that parents will not seek to minimize or discount their feelings' reality, nor will they knowingly allow others to do so. Parents who protect their children provide clear boundaries and expectations within which children can safely operate.

5. Discipline Children test established boundaries. Fallen human nature will do fallen things. When this occurs, parents take on the role of disciplinarians. The word disciple means teach. The ultimate goal of parental discipline is to teach children how to live successfully and independently as adults. Hebrews 12:5-6 declares: "My child, don't ignore it when the Lord disciplines you, and don't be discouraged when he corrects you. For the Lord disciplines those he loves, and he punishes those he accepts as his children" (NLT). A failure to lovingly discipline children is damaging in that it teaches children to be manipulative. There is an appropriate sense of guilt that accompanies the violation of a known standard. Confession and repentance alleviates the guilt. When there is no discipline for the wrong done, there is no resolution of the guilt.

6. <u>Comfort</u> Children get skinned knees and bumps on the head as a normal part of being a child. In many families, it is not okay to cry. It is seen as weakness. God is called "the God of all comfort." Therefore, He knows of our need to be ministered to when we are hurt. Something as simple as "kissing a boo-boo" or rocking a crying child helps to sooth and comfort pain. Likewise, when a child is disciplined, there needs to be reconciliation between the parent and the child. This is a form of comfort that communicates grace and mercy in conjunction with justice.

7. <u>Guidance</u> Particularly in adolescent and young adult children, there is a need for guidance. Many perplexities challenge growing children, and obtaining wise counsel from parents is an invaluable form of love. How many adolescents can go to their parents and tell them anything, even mistakes and problems, and know that they will not be condemned but unconditionally loved and heard? If done wisely, guidance helps children develop decision-making skills. Allowing children to make choices in an age-appropriate way promotes their development, and ultimately their success as adults.

We have stated previously that as parents, we stand in God's place to our children. They begin to understand and appreciate who God is as we fulfill their basic needs. In families with active addictions, the child's capacity to understand God is seriously impaired by the negative view they have of their parent figures. This phenomenon occurs when children transfer their perceptions of their earthly parents onto their heavenly Father.

Diagram 3

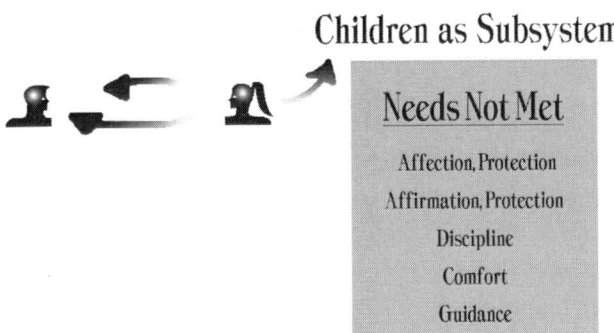

Children as Subsystem

Needs Not Met

Affection, Protection
Affirmation, Protection
Discipline
Comfort
Guidance

Continuing the discussion of the addictive family, the father, in bondage to "A," is unable to fulfill his God-given role. The mother, in her attempt to regain what has been lost in their relationship, is also unavailable to the children. The children begin to develop feelings of bitterness, and in their hearts judge their parents harshly for not meeting their basic needs. We frequently work with people who have never had their basic physical and emotional needs fulfilled by either parent. Until they meet Jesus, they are doomed to a lifetime of searching to find someone to meet these needs.

Four cardinal rules operate in a dysfunctional environment such as the one described above. They are "don't talk, don't feel, don't trust, be perfect." These rules are sometimes, but not always, articulated by either parent: "Don't you dare tell anyone what is going on this house" or, "Your dad didn't mean what he said." Consequently, the children learn that it is not safe to talk about or trust their feelings and that it is unsafe to share whatever feelings are generated by the dysfunction in the family. Being perfect has to do with being a "perfect" little adult. Many a childhood has been lost because the message is that is not okay be be a child.

Sixteen-year-old Ronald had difficulty talking about his feelings and did not trust adults. His mother had been a neglectful, abusive alcoholic and drug addict until he was ten. After that she joined the church and became, in his perception, a religion addict. During her "addictions," she would frequently leave Ronald and his younger sister with babysitters and other family members.

Mom met and married an alcoholic, and Ronald remembers the fights and beatings he and his mother took from her husband. He recalled his mother often saying to him, "Don't tell anyone what goes on here in this house, because it's nobody's business." He was also frequently reminded that, in order to keep the peace, it was best not to say or do anything while his stepfather was around. When Ronald would ask his mother about leaving the abusive situation, his mom would agree to do so and then change her mind. Sometimes Ronald and his mother would leave for a few days and then return. Ronald concluded that he could not trust adults, but neither could he trust his mother's God who seemed so powerless to protect him. As a result, the rules "don't talk, don't feel, and don't trust" were deeply rooted in Ronald at an early age.

With the progressive breakdown in the family, these children are deeply wounded because their needs are unmet. As a result of this wounding, they have many feelings that frequently go unexpressed. These feelings are as

Cleansing the Sanctuary of the Heart

varied as they are many. Some feelings frequently identified are anger, shame, abandonment, loneliness, rage, and feeling unlovable, unwanted, isolated, abused, unprotected, sad, or frustrated. The list is limitless. Since these children learn early that it is not safe to express these feelings, they put them into what we have labeled "the garbage can," with the lid tightly sealed. See Diagram Four. The "garbage can" represents the true condition of our hearts. Instead of thriving, these children learn to survive life. When they grow up and become converted, they cannot internalize the truth of the words of Jesus that say, "I come that they might have life, and that they might have it more abundantly" (John 10:10 KJV).

Diagram 4

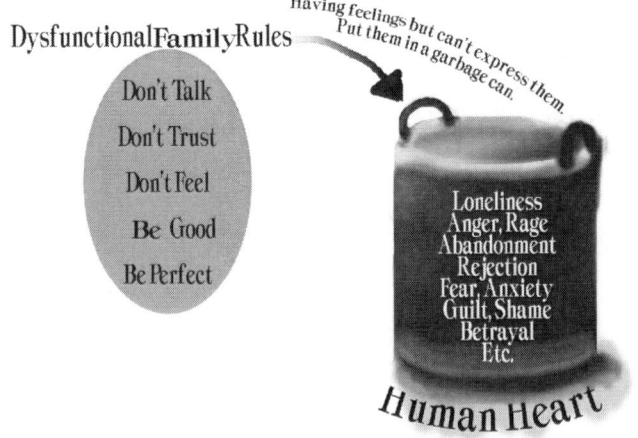

Because of the sinful nature that we all inherit and are subject to before conversion, these children respond bitterly to these childhood experiences. In other words, they sin against their parents by judging them as untrustworthy, unloving, weak, angry, harsh, critical, or neglectful. Matthew 7:2 warns "For with what judgment ye judge, ye shall be judged: and with what measure ye mete, it shall be measured to you again"(KJV), Their bitter judgments will be measured back to them as life experiences, which will be similar, if not identical, to the judgments they have made.

Romans 2:1 describes the phenomenon succinctly: "… whosoever thou art that judgest: for wherein thou judgest another, thou condemnest thyself; for thou that judgest doest the same things" (KJV). These children will not have honor in their hearts toward their parents, and things will not go well for them in their later lives (Deuteronomy 5:16). Once sins become a habit, as a defense against pain, they become part of the character. For example, when we habitually judge our parents, we become judgmental in character.

These sinful habits are wired into our character, forming what we call "structures of self." These structures are as varied as the feelings generated in this dysfunctional environment. They include, but are not limited to the following: self-dependence ("Since the adults in my life are not dependable, I have to take care of myself"), perceiving oneself as a victim ("Poor me! Ain't it awful? What can I do? I'm powerless and without a choice"), rage-aholism (instead of processing feelings, this person immediately becomes rageful and unreasonable), self-righteousness ("How could this person do such a thing? I would *never* do that!"). Such persons can also be controlling, judgmental, self-focused, and performance-oriented. False beliefs about oneself, other classes of people, and the world also frequently become deeply entrenched in the minds and hearts of those raised in dysfunctional families.

I (David) was raised in a home where my father was addicted to control. It was not acceptable for us to make mistakes. We believed that we had to look and be better than everyone else. I responded to this by encasing my humanity in a shell of piety. I would not let myself feel or do anything "bad." I would beat myself mercilessly for the least mistake. If I was not perfect, I was no good at all. I entered the seminary to study for the priesthood in an attempt to live out the role I had assumed of the "perfect one." I was voted the model seminarian. The spiritual director there, noticing my rigid self-control, told me that I needed to relax and even suggested that it would be good for me to swear once in a while. In denying my humanity, I had become my own "god" and was living in the ethereal world of self-righteousness.

The first step to healing for me was to be willing to come down from this pedestal by embracing my humanity. I had to accept that I was not perfect and that it was okay to make mistakes. I had a false belief that if I made a mistake, I would be condemned to hell by God. I had to renounce this false belief. I have a deep appreciation for how difficult it is for those who wear a cloak of religiosity to have a true conversion and religious experience. The structures that I had to be willing to surrender were being in control of myself, controlling others, performance orientation, self-victimization, judgmentalism, self-righteousness, and playing "god." It was extremely helpful to realize that God loved me just as I was, and that He did not want me to perform for Him, but simply to receive His ability to do right and to make me righteous "in Him."

Children in dysfunctional families often learn to medicate their painful feelings. They may initially experience comfort from their medicators, but what begins as comfort often becomes a web of addiction. These addictions may be to drugs, food, alcohol, sex, pornography, television, gambling, religion, gaming, people, or an endless host of other possibilities. By far the greatest addictive bondage all of us have is to self.

Diagram 5

Stuctures I Build To Survive

1. Controlling
2. Self Dependent
3. Performance Oriented
4. Victim/Victimizer
5. Conflict Avoidance
6. Noble Martyr
7. Addictive Behavior
8. Codependent Behavior
9. Self Righteousness
10. Judgementalism

Our family in this illustration is, at best, just surviving. As the father gets deeper into his addiction, the mother finds herself "addicted" to him. The term "codependent" is used to describe the phenomenon by which the spouse becomes addicted to the addict. Codependency is a term used to describe a cluster of behaviors that a person adopts in a relationship with an addict. The wife will attempt to control, manipulate, and even at times join her husband in his addiction in an effort to regain what she perceives as something lost from their relationship. Likewise, each of the children will respond to this dysfunctional situation by assuming equally distinct addictive roles in the family. These roles are types of structures the children build. Often, the older children will assume a parental role over the younger ones. In some cases, they will function as parents for the parent, an extreme example of role reversal.

One young woman we worked with, Earlene, was the oldest of three children. Her father, an alcoholic, began sexually abusing her at a young age. Her mother continued to stay in the marriage despite the abuse she and the children endured. Earlene remembers herself preparing food for the younger children and making sure that they were ready to go to school. One critical memory she had as a five-year-old was that of her mother coming into her room one evening to ask her if she, Mom, should start birth control pills because she didn't want to have any more children. Earlene remembers encouraging her mother to do so because she did not want any other children to be molested the way she was. Although this is an extreme example of the child functioning as the adult and parent, it happens all the time in these dysfunctional homes.

The Cycle of Family Dysfunction
Deuteronomy 5:9

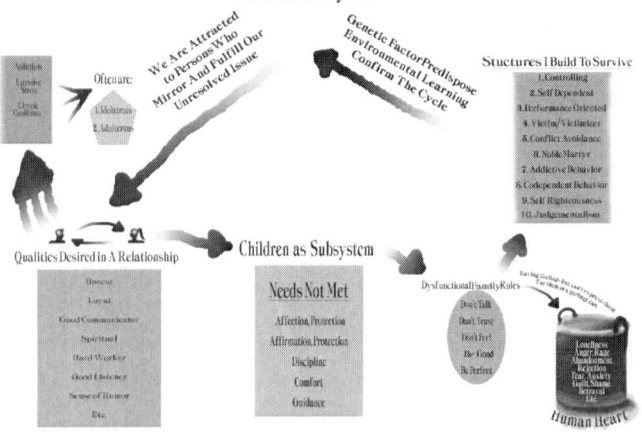

Because children do not perceive that they can be who they are, they assume various roles in order to survive. There are many roles, but the most frequently described are the family hero, the scapegoat, the mascot, and the lost child. These roles are not static, and each child may assume a separate role or more than one role at any given point in time in the family system. These roles are coping mechanisms that help the child to survive a very painful, and often chaotic, life within the family system.

The family hero is often the child who wins strokes and approval by success in some aspect of life: school, sports, and/or job. The family hero will often be one that the family can point to as being the "Pride and Joy" of the family. As a child, I (Beverly) always did well in school, and because I preferred being away from home, I even asked to attend summer school in order to fill my days. My father was a gambler and my mother was continually trying to make ends meet when Dad was out on one of his binges. I continued to excel in school, eventually becoming the first family member to attend and graduate from college. My education was a great source of pride to me as well as to my mother. However, it was also my medicator, my way of escaping the pain of my family life.

The scapegoat often is considered the troublemaker in the family. As the "black sheep," scapegoats are blamed for the problems of the entire family. Professionals consider them to be the "symptom-carrier" of the family. The acting out is generally considered a symptom of the dysfunction in the family. Donita, a 13-year-old from an addictive family, was a compliant child until around the age of twelve, when she began to be blatantly disrespectful to her mother and stepfather, refusing to heed any family rules. Later on, she began acting out at a boarding academy and was subsequently expelled. When she came to us, we enabled her to see her behavior in the context of her family. It was easier for her to take responsibility for her actions and feelings and repent of her sinful responses when she knew that she was not responsible for everything that the family sought to ascribe to her.

The mascot of the family often draws attention away from the "problem" by humor or sickness. These individuals tend to carry the pain of the family as if it were their own. Kevin was such an individual. Full of suppressed rage at his father's addiction and subsequent neglect, he covered his own pain and that of the family by keeping the family in stitches. For years he would not acknowledge his feelings, but would hide in unhealthy relationships with women, which always ended in failure. Healing began only when he had the courage to acknowledge the truth about his feelings.

The lost child is in a world of his own. His coping mechanism is to become oblivious to the craziness of the family by withdrawing into a make-believe world that he can control. In the safety of his world, he becomes super-independent, in charge of everyone and everything. Janet was raised in a home where her alcoholic father was also a rage-aholic. She was a beautiful Christian woman, but she always avoided confrontation. An executive secretary at a local law firm, she felt like running whenever she perceived her boss to be confrontational about her job performance. By reading romance novels compulsively, she retreated into her own imaginary world, a world of fantasy where everyone got along. It got so bad that she brought them to work to read, further exacerbating the problem with her boss.

One thing is clear: the problem is not just with the "addict." The entire family is in pain and has become dysfunctional. They are all in bondage and in need of help. Without the intervention of God and other caring people, the family system will stay in chaos and the cycle of sin will continue to the third and the fourth generation (Deuteronomy 5:9).

There are many solutions to family addiction. Certainly, education, because it helps us to see the problem, is important. Identifying our feelings is also helpful.

Cleansing the Sanctuary of the Heart

Many of us who have stuffed our feelings into a "garbage can" for years are functioning with only half of our human capacities. However, the essence of the problem is not a lack of education or stuffed feelings. Therapies that limit themselves to these areas do not begin to address the root of the problem.

From a Christian perspective, the problem must also be addressed as one of sin and self. Not only have we sinned personally by bitterly judging and not honoring our parents, but we may also have been affected by the sins of the preceding generations. Deuteronomy 5:9-10 identifies how the sins of the fathers are passed along to the third and fourth generations. It is clear that this principle is at work when families with addictions are studied over several generations.

What is the solution for both personal and generational sin? Scripture assures us that "the blood of Jesus Christ cleanseth us from *all* sin" (1 John 1:7, KJV, author's emphasis). But how do we tear down the structures that we have built to protect ourselves, the structures that are now compromising our relationships with others, and even more important, our relationship with God? The Scriptural answer is to die to self: "I am crucified with Christ: nevertheless I live; yet not I but Christ lives in me: and the life which I now live in the flesh I live by the faith of the Son of God who loved me and gave himself for me" (Galatians 2:20, KJV). Scripture exhorts us to "(Cast) down every high thing that exalteth itself against the knowledge of God" (2 Corinthians 10:5, KJV). The cycle of dysfunction can be broken for those who receive by faith the power of the blood of Christ to work in their hearts and lives to cleanse them from all unrighteousness. Death to self is next to impossible without the healing of wounds first. It is the desire of God's heart to both heal the wounds and to bring the cycle to an end by a "death to self" experience in children who have lived in families where active addiction has been present.

Healing Childhood Abuse

Hidden beneath addiction we frequently see the dark secret of abuse. Many addicts who struggle to maintain sobriety do so because they have not allowed God and his healing partners on earth to comfort the pain at the root of their addiction. This is a delicate topic for many reasons. First, the natural tendency is to repress the memory of painful experiences (more on that later). When memories begin breaking forth into the light of awareness, we question whether these things really happened. How could I think such a thing of my parents or others in my life? One of the primary mechanisms of survival when abuse occurs is to deny that it ever occurred. Aside from complete repose in the arms of the Lord after abuse occurs, the options, apart from denial of the abuse, are some form of revenge or total mental collapse.

The life of an abused person is troubled with a deep sense of shame and defectiveness. Always lurking below the surface of awareness is a depression, a desire to die, and a seething anger. Physical symptoms such as headaches, backaches, arthritis, cancer, ulcers, and colitis are frequently associated with unresolved pain from childhood abuse. A recent on study conducted by the Center for Disease Control in conjunction with Kaiser Permanente Hospital interviewed and studied the medical records of over seventeen-thousand patients.[6] They studied the impact of eight adverse childhood experiences (ACEs) on the physical and emotional health of adults in later life. The adverse childhood experiences studied included children exposed to physical abuse, psychological abuse, sexual abuse, domestic violence, living with a family member who is a substance abuser, mentally ill, or suicidal, and having a primary family member in prison. The study revealed that patients with one or more of these factors in their history suffered from alcoholism, illicit drug addiction, chronic obstructive pulmonary disease (COPD), depression, ischemic heart disease, liver disease, risk for intimate partner violence, multiple sexual partners, sexually transmitted diseases, smoking, suicide attempts, and unintended pregnancies. The greater the number of ACEs experienced, the higher the probability for at-risk behavior. One of the most striking findings of the study was that telling a person's story for even fifteen minutes had a therapeutic benefit that lasted for months. The study recommended having children tell their story as soon as possible after the wound occurs. Another remarkable finding was that time did not heal. The negative effects were just as strong fifty years after wounding as they were immediately after the abuse.

Discoveries in neuroscience give us additional clues of the importance of telling our story. When a person tells her story and is truly heard and understood, both she and the listener undergo actual changes in their brain circuitry. They feel a greater sense of emotional and relational connection, decreased anxiety, and greater awareness of and compassion for others' suffering. Even though we cannot change the events of our story, we can change the way our brains are wired. Therefore, we can change the way we experience our story with the tools God has built inside each one of us.[7]

There are many among us, however, who object to the attempt to "dig up the past." They believe that when Paul said to forget those things which are behind, he meant to ignore, repress, or continue to deny that painful events occurred. If I have given my life to Christ, they argue, all of that past has been blotted out. In a sense, they are correct. However, they also fail to take into account that Scripture has much to say about the need to remember, with at least 148 references to the word. Neuroscience again reveals insight into how to apply what Paul meant when he admonishes us to "forget."

Research has shown that the brain has the amazing ability to archive a lifetime of memories. Our sensory organs continually flood us with information-some of it unpleasant and traumatic. We would not get through the day or through life if we did not repress much of it. We have two lines of defense when faced with a traumatic experience: forget that it happened, or given that it happened, reinterpret it in a more positive light.[8] Paradoxically, latest findings from Stanford University suggest that one of the primary function of the brain is to "forget."

Paul's writings suggest that he did not pretend all the events that happened to him after accepting Christ. Philipians 3:8 says: "More than that, I now regard all things as liabilities compared to the far greater value of knowing Christ Jesus my Lord, for whom I have suffered the loss of all things-indeed, I regard them as dung-that I may gain Christ." He reinterpreted them in the light of having relationship with Christ and compared them to waste.

Unfortunately, many abused ones have been so hurt that they do not really trust anyone—not even God—to heal, protect, and love them. For them, if their earthly father hurt them, there is always a nagging fear that their Heavenly Father will do the same thing. Therefore, complete surrender to His arms eludes them. They may want to surrender and choose with their minds to do so, but they are held captive by an evil heart of unbelief (Hebrews 3:12) that creates "divided heart" between what they "know" about God and their experience. They find it difficult to enter into the experience of rest that God desires for His children (Hebrews 3:18).

Again, neuroscience holds some insight to assist us in our understanding of this division. In *Anatomy of the Soul*, Dr. Thompson explains an important brain phenomenon, "For the right hemisphere of the brain, time as such does not exist. The left hemisphere tends to systematically take in all the data that the right hemisphere is transponding to it and logically compare that to what is stored in its neurobiological history."[9] The left brain is all about the past and the future. It "remembers" by neural paths that have previously fired, which then fire more easily again, eventually becoming wired together. Because of these previous firing and wiring together, the future is created. The person may believe, "The Heavenly Father will not protect me like my earthly Father." Or perhaps, "This person reminds me of my father," and automatically reacts as if he is. It is true that we create our future with an eye on the past. The brain is making past connection in the present to manage the future.

This automatic firing is the fertile ground in which roots of bitterness spring up and create trouble in our lives (depression, addictions, and physical problems, to name only a few). They can also defile others in our lives who are important to us (spouse, children, church family, etc.): "...lest any root of bitterness springing up trouble you, *and thereby many be defiled*" (Hebrews 12:15 KJV, italics supplied).

When abuse occurs, there is deep hurt. Whenever we are hurt, there must be a sinful response unless we have the agape love of Jesus. Our fallen human natures and the law of sin and death to which we are subject demand a fallen response. Our natural response is also to protect ourselves by putting up defenses against those who have hurt us. We decide not to be vulnerable to that pain again. Our pain runs to the very core of our beings, as we have seen in the previous section on addiction.

Jesus is still the answer today, but how can He reach the hardened, unbelieving hearts of those who have been so deeply wounded? We work to help a person see that Jesus Himself was touched with the feelings of their infirmities (Hebrews 4:15). Every pain that a wounded one feels was first felt by Jesus. "In all their affliction, he was afflicted" (Isaiah 63:9, NKJV). Throughout His life, He was abused in one way or another. "He is despised and rejected of men; a man of sorrows, and acquainted with grief: and we hid as it were our faces from him; he was despised, and we esteemed him not. Surely he hath borne our griefs and carried our sorrows: yet we did esteem him stricken, smitten of God, and afflicted" (Isaiah 53:3-4, NKJV). As an infant, attempts were made on Jesus' life. His family fled to a foreign country to escape. Jesus lived in Nazareth in poverty. He was derided by the Pharisees because of the circumstances of His conception. He had no home of His own. His ministry was misunderstood by most, including His own disciples. He was betrayed by one of his closest followers. His disciples abandoned Him and ran for their lives. Jesus was hurt in ways difficult for us to comprehend. "While in the guardroom, awaiting His legal trial, He was not protected. The ignorant rabble had seen the cruelty with which He was treated before the council, and from this they took license to manifest all the satanic elements of their nature. Christ's very nobility and godlike bearing goaded them to madness. His meekness, His innocence, His majestic patience filled them with hatred born of Satan. Mercy and justice were trampled upon. Never was a criminal treated in so inhuman a manner as was the Son of God".[10]

After the wounded ones have accepted the possibility that Christ understands because He has lived through abuse too, we invite them to consider that Christ has always been there, has never left them nor forsaken them, even in the midst of their abuse. "For he hath said, I will never leave thee, nor forsake thee" (Hebrews 13:5, KJV). "Through all our trials we have a never-failing Helper. Though He is hidden from mortal sight, the ear of faith can hear His voice saying, Fear not; I am with you. 'I am He that liveth, and was dead; and, behold, I am alive forevermore'" (Rev. 1:18, KJV). "I have endured your sorrows, experienced your struggles, encountered your temptations. I know your tears; I also have wept. The griefs that lie too deep to be breathed into any human ear, I know. Think not that you are desolate and forsaken. Though your pain touches no responsive chord in any heart on earth, look unto Me, and live."[11]

Jesus has often shown wounded ones exactly how He protected them during the actual abuse. He has shown how Satan wanted to hurt them seriously or even take their lives, but how God has, in His mercy, taken most of the blow. Many Christians who have been abused are angry with God for permitting the abuse to happen. Their questions go something like this: "If You are everywhere, know everything, and are all powerful, then You knew what was going to happen before it did and You could have prevented it. Why didn't You? Do You like to see innocent children abused?" Harsh and judgmental are the sentiments in the heart of one who has been a victim of abuse. Asking why abuse was permitted is like asking why sin was permitted. God never wanted sin, because sin hurts the creatures He loves. However, God allows all of His creatures to exercise freedom of choice, including a choice to abuse others. God understands this process of anger. Even though the anger is largely misguided, it is an expression of intimacy. God is big enough to handle whatever emotions we feel that are directed toward Him. He would rather have His children be genuine with Him than to pretend that there is a relationship that really does not exist.

It is our firm conviction that many who allow God to heal them of the pain of abuse, and the sin (and selfish desire) connected to it, are going to be incredibly strong soldiers for Christ in the last days. This thought may not be of much comfort during the time of trial, but nonetheless, it is one of the ways in which the abuse can "work together" for their good.

As the abused ones experience Jesus walking through the valley of the shadow of death with them, the experience of Jesus' agape love warms and softens their hard, self-protecting hearts. They receive the courage to die to all the self-protecting structures that they have built, a true dying to self. They ask that their stony hearts be taken away and that soft hearts be given them. Having been crucified, they too become capable of agape love toward their perpetrators. Just as Jesus cried on the cross, "Father, forgive them," so the abused also choose to forgive all, and are empowered by God to do so.

Those who are abused must find a safe place in which to heal. First, they must be able to trust that they will not be abused again. Unfortunately, we have heard too often that leaders in the church who should be safe are not, and have abused those who have come to them for counsel.

Others who have been well-meaning have discounted the devastation caused by abuse and have given simplistic advice for a complex problem. Often those who have been sexually abused become specific targets for demonic harassment or develop dissociative identity disorder or a personality disorder. Too many in our churches use pious legalisms to beat those who have already been beaten. Bruised reeds are not only broken, but crushed.

God intends that our churches be safe places where support is received when it is needed. At the same time, abused ones need to know that someone loves them enough to be honest with them about their responsibility in the healing process. While those who are abused need compassion, they do not need to be pitied and treated as helpless victims. God never deals with us that way. Neither does He want us to perpetuate this victim cycle in other unhealthy church members. The balance between compassion and confrontation comes from prayer for wisdom from on High. God knows just what a person needs when he needs it. As we sincerely pray for such wisdom, God never fails to give it.

The Personal Healing Touch of Jesus

When we have been deeply hurt, God knows that our capacity to trust Him is greatly diminished. He knows that those who have been abused are not able to believe His word alone. Like Thomas, they doubt God. Therefore, in the beginning of His ministry to them, He will give them personal evidence of His presence. Because they cannot yet trust Him without physical evidence, God will give certain experiences to build their faith. Often such a ministry has been accomplished in our presence through prayer, and sometimes it has been accomplished through an interaction between the person alone and the Holy Spirit. Sometimes the person is given a mental picture of himself as a wounded child. At other times, someone else is given a picture for that person. Other times no picture is given at all. Some persons have been given these pictures long before the counseling process begins. Still others do not even know that the child within is lost and that it needs to be found.

Jesus, through the ministry of the Comforter, is able to transcend both time and space. He is the same yesterday, today, and forever. Therefore, His ministry is not to the adult only, but to the long hidden child of the past, the child within. Jesus was there when we were hurt, and He is always willing to touch us where we were hurt in the past. Beverly and I have frequently been privileged to see Him administer this healing gift. At times, He has given the wounded person a picture of a childhood experience and has shown Himself coming, never without permission, to comfort that one. At other times, no picture has been given; rather, a healing power has come from the word of God when it was spoken to that person. God uses many methods to teach the lesson of His love. He has spoken to the hearts of our guests as they have walked through the woods alone. He has sent hummingbirds at a time of year when there are no hummingbirds. He has sent angels to speak personally to some of our clients. He has given visions and dreams. He has done whatever the person has needed.

Typically, Jesus seeks and finds us in the areas of our deepest wounding, just as He searched for the lost sheep in the parable. For example, Maureen, adopted at infancy, saw herself as a newborn in a steel crib in a sterile white room with no blankets or toys. Brian was coerced into heavy labor for long hours from the age of six. He saw himself as a little boy, aged eight or nine, hiding in the woods. When Jesus found him, he did not want to go with Him because he was afraid he would be put back to work again. Heidi saw herself as a little girl outside her room hiding on the roof. The thought of Jesus taking her back into the house was terrifying to her because it was in her room that her father had repeatedly molested her as a little girl. Connie's father had wanted a boy, and he let that be known during the first few years of her life. She saw herself as a four-year-old little girl who had secreted herself in a garden because it was not okay for her to be a girl.

When Jesus finds the child within the wounded one, the person must first give Him permission to comfort that child. The person must experience the presence of Jesus as safe before giving this permission. When permission is given, the person often experiences Jesus picking him up, holding him, sitting him on His lap, or taking some similar comforting action. The pictures that God often gives are powerful, personal expressions of loving ministry to the wounded one exactly how it is needed. According to Scriptural promise and example, this image of Jesus is appropriate:

> For the Lord shall comfort Zion: he will comfort all her waste places; and he will make her wilderness like Eden, and her desert like the garden of the Lord; joy and gladness shall be found therein, thanksgiving, and the voice of melody.
>
> (Isaiah 51:3, KJV).

> Therefore, the redeemed of the Lord shall return, and come with singing unto Zion; and everlasting joy shall be upon their head: they shall obtain gladness and joy; and sorrow and mourning shall flee away. I, even I, am he that comforteth you.
>
> (Isaiah 51:11-12, KJV)

> When my father and my mother forsake me, then the Lord will take me up.
>
> (Psalm 27:10, KJV)

> The Lord doth build up Jerusalem: he gathereth together the outcasts of Israel. He healeth the broken in heart, and bindeth up their wounds.
>
> (Psalms 147:2-3, KJV)

We have found it essential when praying for wounded ones to use Scriptures such as these because power is in the Word of God to accomplish what it says. When we pray, we always pray with words of confidence and faith. Christian counselors must know who they are in Christ and be warriors, mighty men and women of valor, on behalf of those who are weak. We have found it helpful to paint visual pictures when praying for healing of wounds. Just as Jesus spoke in parables that the people of His time could relate to, we use similar imagery (flowers, ice, light, heat) when attempting to connect counselees with spiritual realities such as the healing of the spirit, newness of life, the breaking of spiritual bonds, and so forth. The Scriptures are filled with word pictures such as those in Isaiah 51:3.

Wounded ones must always be brought to the place where they are willing to forgive those who have hurt them, to ask forgiveness for their fallen responses to the wounding, and to ask that the structures they have built to survive the pain of life be brought to death. Where there has been a profound wounding of the spirit, there must be a call to renewal of life, prayer for the separation of their spirit from that of their abuser, prayer for protection from the enemy, and a rooting and grounding in the love of God. We cannot emphasize enough that God always hears and answers such prayers on behalf of His wounded children. "In all their affliction he was afflicted" (Isaiah 63:9, KJV). He knows, He hears, He heals.

God's power to heal is just as real today as it was in the days when Jesus walked the earth.

No matter how painful the experience of your life, the power of Christ is available to you. Will you receive it?

Chapter 4

The Law of Love: God's Antidote for Sin

"Ye have heard that it hath been said, Thou shalt love thy neighbor, and hate thine enemy. But I say unto you, Love your enemies, bless them that curse you, do good to them that hate you, and pray for them which despitefully use you, and persecute you; that ye may be the children of your Father which is in heaven: for he maketh his sun to rise on the evil and on the good, and sendeth rain on the just and on the unjust. For if you love them which love you, what reward have ye? do not even the publicans the same? And if ye salute your brethren only, what do ye more than others? do not even the publicans so? Be ye therefore perfect, even as your Father which is in heaven is perfect."

(Matthew 5:43–48, kjv*)*

The keynote of this passage from Matthew is love; the keynote of the parallel passage from Luke is mercy: "Be ye therefore merciful, as your Father also is merciful" (Luke 6:36, KJV). Therefore, it would appear that "perfection," the character of the Father, has both love and mercy as characteristics. Love and mercy are attributes, or virtues, of the mature, or "perfect" Christian life. The Greek word for the type of love referred to in these passages is "agape." This type of love is not natural to the human being, but comes as a gift from God. It is not natural for us to love our enemies. Paul talks about the possibility of a man giving his life for another good man. However, God demonstrated His love by dying for us while we were still His enemies (see Romans 5:5-8, KJV). "Greater love hath no man than this, that a man lay down his life for his friends" (John 15:13, KJV).

Laying down our lives is not just dying a physical death as in martyrdom. Today God wants His people to be a "living sacrifice" (Romans 12:1, KJV). The loving death He wants us to die for one another is a self-sacrificing love that seeks the good of the other. Unfortunately, Jesus sadly says of too many of us Christians: "But I know you, that ye have not the love *of God* in you" (John 5:42, KJV, author's emphasis). Notice that Jesus did not say: "You have not the love *for God* in you." His pain was that we do not receive the gift that God wants to give us. Jesus knows that we are incapable of giving agape love. It is the purpose of this chapter to explore this kind of love as compared with human love, and suggest the way to open ourselves to receive this gift of love from God.

We have entitled this chapter "The Law of Love." It may seem strange to some that love would be described as a law, so let us illustrate. All law is connected to government. If there were no government anywhere, there would be no law. Government is that which is legislated by a governing body or person. So in this world we have kings with their kingdoms, republics with their elected officials, and so forth. The purpose of these leaders is to govern. God has a kingdom also, although it is not of this world. It is a spiritual kingdom and a heavenly one. As with any other kingdom, God's kingdom has a government and laws by which it operates. Ellen White comments:

> "The law of love being the foundation of the government of God, the happiness of all intelligent beings depends upon their perfect accord with its great principles of righteousness. God wants from all His creatures the service of love—service that springs from an appreciation of His character. He takes no pleasure in forced obedience; and to all He grants freedom of will that they may render Him voluntary service. While all created beings acknowledged the allegiance of love, there was perfect harmony throughout the universe of God. While love to God was supreme, love for one another was confiding and unselfish." [1]

The following statement is even more descriptive of this law of love:

> "In the light shining from Calvary it will be seen that the law of self-renouncing love is the law of life for earth and heaven; that the love

which 'seeketh not her own' has its source in the heart of God; and that in the meek and lowly One is manifested the character of Him who dwelleth in the light which no man can approach unto…The angels of glory find their joy in giving—giving love and tireless watch care to souls that are fallen and unholy. Looking unto Jesus, we see that it is the glory of our God to give. 'I do nothing of Myself,' said Christ; 'I seek not Mine own glory,' but the glory of Him that sent Me. (John 8:28; 6:57; 8:50; 7:18 KJV). In these words is set forth the great principle which is the law of life for the universe. All things Christ received from God, but He took to give. So in the heavenly courts, in His ministry for all created beings: through the beloved Son, the Father's life flows out to all; through the Son it returns, in praise and joyous service, a tide of love, to the great Source of all. And thus through Christ the circuit of beneficence is complete, representing the character of the great Giver, the law of life. In heaven itself this law was broken. Sin originated in self-seeking."[2]

The passages above express the essential nature of the government of heaven; God desires that this government be realized on earth. In heaven, the law of love is the law of life. Life in heaven is an expression of divine love. On earth, happiness depends upon our living in accord with this law of love. This type of love is described as self-renouncing and self-sacrificing, seeking the happiness and good of another even when there is sacrifice to self involved. It cannot be forced; it must be chosen freely. This love was given by the Father to the Son and in return, given by the Son to the Father. It was given by the angels to God and by the angels to man. God loves man and desires man's free love in return. Jesus, in quoting from Deuteronomy 6:5, says: "Thou shalt love the Lord thy God with all thy heart, and with all thy soul, and with all thy mind. This is the first and great commandment" (Matthew 22:37-38, KJV). God not only wants us to love Him but to express this love to one another: "And the second is like unto it, Thou shalt love thy neighbor as thyself" (Matthew 22:39, KJV). In fact, we are taught in very strong language that love for our brother is an expression of our love for God: "If a man say, I love God, and hateth his brother, he is a liar: for he that loveth not his brother whom he hath seen, how can he love God whom he hath not seen?" (1 John 4:20, KJV). If love for our neighbor is absent, we do not love God even if we say we do.

Let us take these principles and apply them in a practical way to our lives. We have seen that Jesus said that the mark of a true Christian is that he loves not only his friends but his enemies also. When we examine our hearts, we discover who our enemies truly are. A friend is one whom we welcome into intimate relationship with ourselves. We are comfortable with our friends. We like being in the company of friends. In fact, we would rather be with them than with anyone else. We do not need to put up defenses to protect ourselves from our friends. Though they are human and make mistakes, we accept them that way. We do not build up walls between us and our friends. We feel able to be ourselves in their presence.

When we look realistically at our relationships with those who have hurt us, we see that we are not comfortable in their presence. We retain a nagging fear that they will hurt us again. We build up walls of defense that allow these people to get only so close, even if we live with them. In fact, these walls of defense are often so strong and thick that no communication goes through them; instead, going over these walls are stones of accusation and blame. The truth is that we often view those closest to us as our enemies. We defend against them, fight with them, and often have murder in our hearts against them. Many of us do this while claiming to love God, but as we have seen from Scripture, it is impossible to love God with the hatred for our brother in our hearts (See 1 John 4:20, KJV).

If we apply this discussion to parents who have wounded us, we may see that we view them as enemies too. Our hearts have been turned away from them. But we are told in Malachi 4:5-6 that the work of the church just before the second coming of Christ is to "turn the heart of the fathers to the children, and the heart of the children to their fathers…" (KJV). The ministry of reconciliation is not meant to occur between man and God only, but also between all men, even those whom we have in our hearts considered our enemies.

Many have asked: How is it possible to love those who have molested, raped, beaten, and abused me? Without the experience of agape love, it is impossible to love our "enemies," especially those who have been our "friends" (see Psalm 55:12-14, KJV). To begin answering this question, we will contrast human love with God's love. Figure One illustrates this contrast:

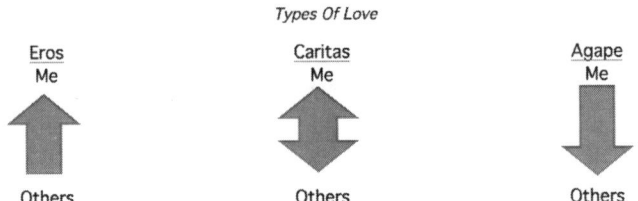

The word "Eros" is a Greek word designating "self-love." Eros is the root of the word erotic. This type of love is typical of an infants whose experience is that they are the center of the universe. All others (parents, siblings, etc.) exist to meet their needs. The human infant is the most helpless of all creatures. A baby is totally dependent upon its parents for food, diaper changing, protection, and emotional nurture. Without these things, the infant will die. It is the parents' responsibility to provide for these needs. Parents stand in God's place as providers, protectors, and those who give nurture. When these needs are not met by parents, the child's development is delayed at this infant stage.

We work with many Christians who, as adults, are still seeking the approval and nurture of their parents. Not having received enough approval and nurture from them as infants, they continue seeking these securities as adults. They seek to have these dependency needs met by their parents, a spouse who is a parent figure, by other "mature" adults, or by God. There have been several strong women in my (David's) life that I have used to fill the hole in my life left by a lack of nurture from my parents. I was a little boy seeking the approval of a "mother," and I overlooked many glaring faults and inconsistencies in these relationships. I was unable to set limits, so consequently, I hurt them and myself, also causing grief to many others who saw the problem clearly and wanted to help.

Many marriages suffer when one partner is invested in being a parent and the other is delayed at this Eros stage of development. Even in our religious experience we look at God or at our church as entities whose job it is to meet our needs. This need for approval and love leads many into cults where authoritarian leaders promise a sheltered, stable, nurturing experience. In our experience, many who have issues with the church as an organization really have unresolved issues with their mothers.

The truth is that many of us are infants emotionally; we are self-centered, believing in our hearts that others exist to meet our needs. A friend has humorously suggested that we often grow from infancy in "Pampers" into adulthood using "Depends." We have never put away the childish things (1 Corinthians 13:11). Figure 2 illustrates the self-focus of the Eros heart.

Self-focused Love

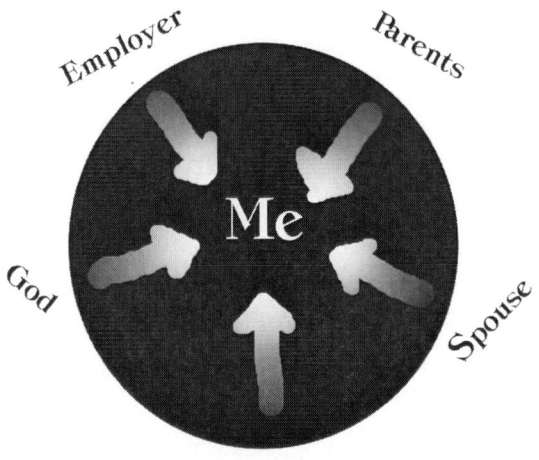

The second type of human love can be called "Caritas." Here there is a mixture of self-love and self-sacrificing love. It is love with strings or conditions attached to it. In this type of love, marriage is seen as a contract in which each partner is expected to give his share. The contract states: "If I do not get my 'share' from my partner, I am justified in withholding my share." This type of love takes offense when real or imagined wrong is done. Sex may be withheld, or silence may be used as a punishment. There are many similarities between the commonly used term "codependency" and caritas love. Although a complete elaboration of the syndrome of codependency is beyond the scope of this book, a brief definition will suffice. Codependency is a set of maladaptive, compulsive behaviors learned by family members. These behaviors are developed to survive in a family that is experiencing great emotional pain and stress. These maladaptive behaviors result in an overreaction to things outside of us and an underreaction to things inside of us.

Codependents are wonderful caretakers. They find it much easier to give than to receive. However, all of their giving has expectations attached to it. They expect recognition, if not from the person who is the object of their addictive love, then from others who will see their noble, martyr-like efforts at rescuing this lost person. Codependents get their strokes from being in a dysfunctional relationship with one that they can "love." This love is not pure, although it appears very much to be self-sacrificing. Caritas love, the very best that human beings can generate, is really a counterfeit of agape love. The only difference is in the motive of the person who loves. In agape love, the sacrifice is pure, while in caritas, self is alive and well, seeking to feel justified, superior, or righteous through the act of loving. Figure 3 illustrates "me" in the center of my world giving to others but expecting something in return. In order to determine the type of love you demonstrate, you may ask yourself the following questions: What is it that you expect in relationships? Do you feel offended when you do not get it? Are you willing to surrender your right to expect these things?

Conditional Love

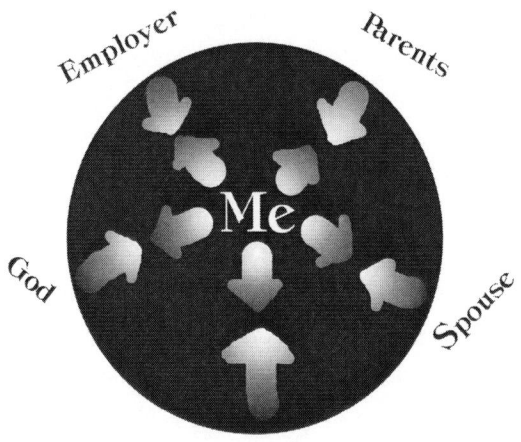

In true agape love, however, there are no strings attached. It flows from me to the other even when that person offends me, hurts me, or is my enemy. The model for this type of love is Jesus: "Herein is love, not that we loved God, but that he loved us" (1 John 4:10 KJV). He did not initiate this love after we were His friends, but while we were still His enemies. "But God demonstrates His own love toward us, in that while we were yet sinners, Christ died for us" (Romans 5:8 KJV). Likewise, Paul said of himself: "And I will very gladly spend and be spent for you; though the more abundantly I love you, the less I be loved" (2 Corinthians 12:15, KJV). We are counseled to do the same (1 John 4:11). A person having this kind of love does not blame or accuse when there is a conflict, but rather asks: "How did I contribute to this problem? What in me needs to die?" Agape love stops all demands that the other change. It surrenders its "rights." An objective examination reveals that both parties in most conflicting interactions have responsibility. However, the person with agape love never looks at the fault of the other but asks God to search his own heart and show him his deficiencies. Such love goes entirely against our carnal nature, which has been conditioned to blame since the Garden of Eden. Figure 4 illustrates that God is no longer on the outside meeting my needs. I am dead to myself and my life is hidden with Christ in God (Colossians 3:3). I become a wellspring of love toward others with no expectation of getting anything in return.

Other-focused Love

The question remains: "How do I get this agape love if the best that humans can do is love conditionally?" First, this love, as we have seen, is God's love and therefore comes from Him. He pours His love into us. The first fruit of the Holy Spirit is agape love. We receive the capacity for this love, then, when we are born again of the Holy Spirit. The highest expression of agape love was the cross, which signifies that Jesus accepted the possibility of eternal separation from His Father as the consequence for taking on our sin. Romans 6:3-5 states:

> "Or do you not know that all of us who have been baptized into Christ Jesus have been baptized into His death? Therefore we have been buried with Him through baptism into death, in order that as Christ was raised from the dead through the glory of the Father, so we too might walk in newness of life. For if we have become united with Him in the likeness of His death, certainly we shall be also in the likeness of his resurrection" (NASB).

This newness of life is resurrection life, the very divine life of God Himself within us. God within us loves with agape love. When by faith we let God live in us, He loves through us. This love is the result of death and burial of self—the destruction of our "wretched man" (Romans 7:24)—the deliverance from the body of this death.

In practical terms, how do we go from life to death to life again? We ask God to show us all of the counterfeits within us, including the best love that we as human beings can muster. Are you willing to die to your best ability to love, in which is interwoven threads of self? Are you willing to die to your codependent martyr love? Has it ever really brought you the lasting nurture, peace, and rest that you were seeking? If you are willing to surrender these human counterfeits, then place them upon the altar before the Lord and ask Him to bring them to death. Name them specifically. Ask Christ to nail them to the cross. Then by faith believe that He has done what you have asked Him to do. Thereafter, walk by faith in the newness of life that He has given you.

We are empowered by God living within us to choose agape love when faced with unpleasant circumstances. As God's people, we know that persecution is soon to come upon us in this world when we stand for Christ and for His truth. We will choose to love our persecutors and do so empowered by the Holy Spirit. Matthew 5:44 will be fulfilled in our lives: "Love your enemies, bless them that curse you, do good to them that hate you, and pray for them which despitefully use you, and persecute you" (KJV). We will love those who tell us that we cannot buy or sell (Revelation 13:17) or that they will kill us if we do not surrender our faith (Revelation 13:15). This is the meaning of 1 John 4:16-18:

> "And we have known and believed the love that God hath to us. God is love; and he that dwelleth in love dwelleth in God, and God in him. Herein is our love made perfect, that we may have boldness in the day of judgment: because as he is, so are we in this world. There

is no fear in love; but perfect love casteth out fear: because fear hath torment. He that feareth is not made perfect in love." (KJV)

As Jesus was when He was in this world, so are we in this world. Because we love Jesus and our neighbors who need to see Christ in us, we have boldness to live this truth. Our love for Jesus and His love in us for others has cast out all fear of what they will do to us. We are willing to live or die, if only Christ is lifted up.

"And I, if I be lifted up from the earth, will draw all men unto me" (John 12:32 KJV). When we are crucified with Christ, we will be lifted to the cross with Him. When we have died to self, His love will be expressed consistently in us and through us. And men will also be drawn to us because of their experience of Christ's love in us. This love transcends formulas and "how-to" self-help guides. It is nothing less than the working of the Holy Spirit. He tells us what to do and what to say during these difficult times.

Chapter 5

The Height and Depth of Law: What Was Natural Became Unnatural

> "And now, Israel, what does the Lord thy God require of thee, to fear the Lord thy God, to walk in all his ways, and to love him, and to serve the Lord thy God with all thy heart and with all thy soul, to keep the commandments of the Lord, and his statutes, which I command thee this day for thy good?"
>
> *(Deuteronomy 10:12-13, KJV)*

Mountains are awesome! On a recent trip out west, we traveled the Bear Tooth Highway that winds up 11,000 feet of sheer cliff. In the middle of summer, we passed snow by the side of the road. The beauty took our breath away. The law is like those mountains. It cannot be ignored. Its majestic beauty draws us internally like a magnet to metal. Its mountainous presence boldly declares to all, "You cannot ignore me." If a pilot flying in the fog chose to ignore the reality of a mountain because he could not see it, his life and the lives of his passengers would likely be lost. We run the same risk when we ignore the law. Whether our blindness is willful or ignorant, we crash with fearful results.

The universe and all that is in it is governed by law. From the largest macro system in the galaxy to the smallest micro system within the atom, the law of God is written. As Christians, we appreciate the law of God. Our love of God's law is manifested by our obeying His word. For us, keeping the law is not the means to salvation, but the expression of our love for God. "If you love me," Jesus said, "keep My commandments" (John 14:15, KJV).

But even our understanding of the law and how deeply it permeates every facet of human experience is far from complete, especially when it comes to the realm of the soul and spirit.[1] The same principle of law that governs the physical world governs the world of the mind. There are predictable laws that govern every operation of the mind and heart. God's desire was that there would be perfect harmony, the result of obedience to His laws. However, sin entered the universe. Through Lucifer's rebellion, the law of sin and death came into the world, and we are its heirs. "So then with the mind I myself serve the law of God; but with the flesh the law of sin" (Romans 7:25, KJV). A lawbreaker will receive the consequences of a violation of law until he learns the lesson that the consequence was designed to teach. Until we accept salvation in Jesus Christ personally, the law requires our death (Romans 6:23). We are born as children of fallen Adam and under the dominion of Satan. We are born with carnal minds that are not subject to the law of God and are defined as "enmity against God" in the Scriptures (Romans 8:7, KJV). This is what Scripture means by our being subject to the law of sin and death. We must sin. We cannot do anything else until grace intervenes.

The good news is that grace did intervene two-thousand years ago in the person of Jesus Christ. "For the law of the Spirit of life in Christ Jesus hath made me free from the law of sin and death" (Romans 8:2, KJV). But freedom from the law of sin and death does not do away with the law. The universe is still run by law, or else we would all cease to exist. We are simply reestablished under the law of the spirit of life, which was our original condition before sin. The laws which govern human beings for our good (Deuteronomy 10:13) continue, but our response to them is from the new reality of the divine nature rather than from our carnal nature (2 Peter 1:4). Many of us who have been saved by grace do not understand that these laws govern both the conscious and unconscious parts of man. Not having asked forgiveness for unknown sin, even as Christians our lives remain bound to sin's consequences. Perhaps the following illustration will clarify this truth.

Have you ever thought about the law of gravity? It is always in operation and it does not vary. It is not a respecter of persons. We all are subject to it. Is it not reassuring to know that you will not go floating off into outer space? If we were to climb to the top of a three-story building and jump off, we would obviously be subject to the law of gravity. In all likelihood, we would be seriously hurt or killed. What if we were too young to know that there was any such thing as the law of gravity? Does that exempt us from being subject to the law? Let us assume that you have a small baby with you in a house that is on fire. You are both on the second story of the house. You cannot get out except through a second-story window. You decide to risk jumping with your baby. Your baby is too young to know about gravity, but will both of you be subject to this law? Yes, indeed. Not knowing about a law does not make us exempt from its consequences. Just as with gravity, we are subject to the inner laws of our being whether we are aware of them or not. A child will suffer the harmful effects of a poor diet even when he is unaware that there are laws that govern nutrition. Likewise, a child who is unaware of the laws that govern the mind and heart is still affected by a violation of these laws.

Because we are born under the law of sin and death, children who are hurt by their parents, intentionally or otherwise, will sin against them. As children or as adults, whenever we are hurt, we must, by the law of sin at work in us, sin against the one who hurt us if we do not have the love of Jesus as a living reality within. As a result, we develop bitterness and resentment toward those who hurt us. We are slaves to the law of sin (Romans 7:25). Children, who may never have heard of the requirement to honor father and mother, cannot honor a parent who hurts them; therefore, they judge the offender very harshly in their hearts. "You can't be trusted. You don't love me. I hate you." Such thoughts are the unspoken, unconscious sentiments of children who are hurt. They are violations of the law that says: "Honor thy father and thy mother" (Deuteronomy 5:16, KJV). These children have sinned. At this point many ask, "How can God hold the child responsible?" We reply very simply that God does not hold such children accountable in terms of salvation. God is not unfair. He would never punish someone for what they have not knowingly, willfully chosen. While there is no legal condemnation, it is essential to understand that there are required consequences.

A study of Leviticus, Chapters 4 and 5, reveals God's approach to dealing with such sins of ignorance.

> "Now if anyone of the common people sins unintentionally in doing any of the things which the Lord has commanded not to be done, and becomes guilty, or if his sin, which he has committed, is made known to him, then he shall bring his offering, a goat, a female without defect, for his sin which he has committed." (Leviticus 4:2728, KJV)

God cannot excuse sin of any kind regardless of how "innocent" the sinner may appear. "The wages of sin is death" (Romans 6:23, KJV). Sin requires the death penalty. There are no exceptions. Therefore, the ignorant sinner was instructed to bring a female kid goat without blemish for a sacrifice. This goat without blemish typified Christ, the spotless sacrifice who was slain for the sins of the world. Jesus paid the price so that these wounded, sinful children would not die but be saved. Since Jesus paid the price for the sins of these wounded ones, the following scripture appears to apply: "If anyone sees his brother commit a sin that does not lead to death, he should pray and God will give him life. I refer to those whose sin does not lead to death" (1 John 5:16, NIV). The only sins that "lead to death" are those that are committed with no intention of asking forgiveness or turning away from the sin. Consider the difference between Judas and Peter. Both sinned grievously, but Judas' sin led to eternal death because his repentance was not based on a sacrificial love for Jesus. Peter's heart was broken by his sin, and he was restored (See John 21).

While hurt children are not subject to the condemnation of death, a violation of the law always carries with it a consequence. The law in question here is the law of judging. For example, Jesus said: "Judge not, that ye be not judged. For with what judgment ye judge, ye shall be judged: and with what measure ye mete, it shall be measured to you again" (Matthew 7:1, 2 KJV). The consequence of violating the law of judging is that "what goes around comes around." A person will get back whatever he measures out. That is the law. Therefore, a wounded one who judges his parents bitterly is requiring that somehow, sometime in his life he will have difficulty in the same area of judgment. Roots of bitterness spring up and trouble us (Hebrews 12:15). In Mark's case, this law is apparent. Mark was born to a teenage mother. His father spent many of Mark's growing up years in and out of jail. Mark decided at a young age to become a lawyer. After finishing his education, and against the advice of many, he decided to start a private practice. He had difficulty being financially responsible, and at one point in his young marriage, he decided he wanted to leave the marriage. Through counseling, he saw that he had abandoned his family as his father had abandoned his childhood family. Even the choice of his profession was prompted by his bitter judgments of his father. He came to see that he became a lawyer to try to save his father. These attitudes and actions were the lingering consequences of his violation of law.

The propensity to sin is built into our nature (see Ps 51:5, 58:3; Is 48:8b). In addition, we make personal choices to sin in response to the world in which we live. To sin is natural. Even in our best attempts to do good are interwoven the threads of self-seeking, self-protecting sin. We are rebels by birth and by choice. Even as Christians, our choice is often unconscious, driven by our need for self-protection and self-justification. Samantha is one who made such a choice. The older of two girls, Samantha grew up in a Christian home. When her cousins molested her, she told no one. When she grew up and had children of her own, she could not stand the thought of her husband disciplining them. She became hypervigilant, protecting her children to the point that she was often physically exhausted. In counseling she was helped to see that because of the rage associated with her not being protected by her parents, she had taken the role of an all-protecting god in the life of her own children. The consequence in her life was exhaustion, fueled by her unconscious, angry determination not to allow her children to suffer what she suffered.

We learn to love or hate law based upon our experience of our parents' discipline. If we experienced his or her discipline as harsh, rigid, or unfair, we will resent having anyone tell us what to do. If our parents were invested in controlling what we do, believe, or think, we sense their "force" and instinctively rebel against it. Children need to be taught to make their own healthy choices. They need to be taught independent thinking, even if it sometimes leads them to make choices that we would not necessarily make.

The balance to encouraging independent thinking is that a parent's word must be law to the child. Children lose respect for parents who are manipulated into changing what they have said through tantrums, begging, crying, pouting, or outright rebellion. The result is that they learn to believe that God's law does not have to be kept either. Thus, the fear (respect) of the Lord that is the beginning of wisdom is lost. When children choose to violate the law of a parent, they must know that there will always be a consequence. Some parents feel the need to regulate every aspect of their children's lives. This is unwise. It would be better to consistently enforce fewer rules than to inconsistently enforce many rules. The child learns to see the parents' rules as a form of protection rather than as an attempt to keep him from having fun or doing his own thing. It is in the security of law that the child learns to truly think and act independently. When this principle is learned early in life, it is the best safeguard against the child being unduly influenced by peer pressure of any kind later in life.

If parents' rules are too strict, rebellion may be the most constructive choice a child can make. It is nearly impossible for such children to exclaim: "O how I love Thy law! It is my meditation all the day" (Psalms 119:97 KJV). It is likewise difficult for them to understand God's purpose in giving the law. God's purpose in giving us law is that it is for our good (see Deuteronomy 10:12, 13). Law is meant to be a blessing, not a curse or weight to keep us from happiness. When we force our children to comply or when we administer discipline arbitrarily, we are developing in our children a hatred for the law. Their rebellion against authority may include any authority figures such as parents, police, government, and God—the ultimate authority. Margo was such a child. Severely abused, primarily by her father, she had always been a "good" girl growing up. However, from the time that she first learned to drive, she was terrified of police. However, along with her fear came a blatant lack of regard for speed limits. When she was caught for speeding and then alternately break into tears or verbally abuse the police who stopped her. In counseling, we helped her to see that her problem with police directly related to her experience of her father. She was willing to repent of her judgments of her father and was freed from her reaction to police. As stated earlier, such rebellion is often unconscious. We want to do what is right but we find that we cannot (see Romans 7).

A lesson from nature may help us to understand the spiritual concept we have been discussing. Gardeners love to have a weed-free plot so that the vegetables will receive the full benefit of the nutrients in the soil. Therefore, they regularly pull the weeds from the garden. The garden looks perfect, weed-free. The following week, the gardener returns to find weeds growing again. Why have the weeds sprung up again? Most of us would correctly respond that it is because roots were left below the surface. That is how it is with sin also. Known, confessed sin is forgiven. "If we confess our sins, he is faithful and just to forgive us our sins" (1 John 1:9, KJV). This promise is reliable, but how does it apply to unconscious, unknown sin? God does not magically erase the consequences of unconfessed sin. Even though forgiveness was accomplished for everyone on the cross, we need to confess our sins as the Lord reveals them to us in order to be freed from the consequence that sin requires.

Hebrews 4:13 says, "All things are naked and opened unto the eyes of him with whom we have to do" (KJV). He knows every sinful thought and action even if it occurred in a time of our childhood that we cannot remember. However, He not only knows, He also helps.

> "In the same way the Spirit also helps our weakness; for we do not know how to pray as we should, but the Spirit Himself intercedes for us with groanings too deep for words; And He who searches the hearts knows what the mind of the Spirit is, because He intercedes for the saints according to the will of God." (Romans 8:26, 27, NASB)

The Spirit is at work interceding and, when necessary, bringing to our memory those sins that need to be repented of. "Sow to yourselves in righteousness, reap in mercy; break up your fallow ground: for it is time to seek the Lord, till he come and rain righteousness upon you" (Hosea 10:12, KJV). The fallow ground is that of our hearts hardened by years of self-protection. Plowing up the ground of a heart that has been fallow (not broken up) for a long time is a painful thing. The plow must, of necessity, run deep into the unconscious life of the Christian.

The Lord will not rest until the fallow ground of the heart in the life of one of His children has been broken up and become productive. Either that child of God says: "I will allow You to go no further," or everything will be seen, confessed, and forsaken. The job of a Christian counselor is to lovingly point to God's standard of righteousness and to help the person see what he has been unable to see.

The Christian counselor cannot give a "peace and safety" message of comfort and avoid confronting the sin problem; neither can he ignore the damage inflicted by a wound, as unknown to a wounded one as it might be. The Spirit is at work in the heart preparing the way for a Spirit-led counselor to bring "sight to the blind, to set at liberty them that are bruised" by sin (Luke 4:18). This is one of the greatest works that can be done because the battleground between Christ and Satan is for the minds of men and women. "And the dragon was wroth with the woman, and went to make war with the remnant of her seed, which keep the commandments of God, and have the testimony of Jesus Christ" (Revelation 12:17, KJV). Keeping the commandments of God is not primarily an external thing, but a work of the heart, following an assent by the mind. He promises: "I will put my law in their inward parts and write it in their hearts" (Jeremiah 31:33, kjv).

We have seen that there are laws that govern every aspect of our being, including the mind, and that these laws are binding whether we are aware of them or not. There are always consequences connected to a violation of law. Even when I do not know that I have sinned against someone—for example, my parents—the consequences are present and unconsciously being played out in my life. The Holy Spirit is hard at work helping me to see those things I am blind to in myself. He is committed to finishing the work unless I hinder Him. In the next chapter, we will discuss four specific laws that are essential to healthy living. Our responses to these laws determine our life experience.

Chapter 6

The Laws of Honor, Judging, Vows, and Faith: God's Accommodation for Sin

> "They do not understand how far reaching are the claims of the holy law, how intimately the precepts of the law are to be brought into practical life."
>
> Ellen G. White

There are many laws that govern the mind and thus intimately affect the speech, thoughts, and behavior. This chapter will focus on four of the most fundamental, the four which have the most practical implications. These laws touch the very heart of human experience and predict how life will be for all of us.

The Law of Honor

The first fundamental law is found in Deuteronomy 5:16: "Honor your father and your mother, as the Lord your God has commanded you, that your days may be prolonged and that it may go well with you on the land which the Lord your God gives you" (NASB). This commandment, one of the Decalogue, has far-reaching effects on the human experience. It predicts how our life will go in the areas of marriage, relationships of all types (including those within our church family), parenting, and discipline. As counselors, whenever we see a problem in any of these areas, we know where the root of the problem lies. Christian counseling is straightforward when we understand God's laws and how to apply them under the guidance of the Holy Spirit.

In Ephesians 6:2 we are told that Deuteronomy 5:16 is the first commandment with promise. The promises are that if we honor our parents, we will live long lives and our lives will go well. However, if we do not or are not able to honor our parents, we will experience curses or consequences that are just the opposite of the promise or blessing. That is how life works in the context of Deuteronomy 5:16. There is no escaping it. We will live shortened lives and they will not go well. What does this mean in practical terms?

One's life can be shortened by engaging in any activity and having any internal structure that is oriented to death rather than life. Examples include young people who take drugs, commit suicide at record levels, listen to destructive music, drive recklessly, and engage in sexual activity regardless of the danger. However, a shortening of life is not limited to youth. Many of us who carry these types of activities into our adulthood also have internalized patterns of living that are death-oriented, such as a victim structure or a death wish. We are not able to embrace life fully but are condemned to surviving in a self-created world of fear and pain. We wrestle with death. We suppress thoughts of suicide, struggle with depression, and secretly believe that life (our spouse, our children) would be better off without us.

The manifestation of life "not going well" is very specific. We have found that life does not go well for a person in the specific areas in which he or she did not or was not able to honor his or her parents. If my issue involves how poorly I felt provided for, life will not go well for me in the area of finances. In my own life (David), I did not honor my parents in the area of parenting. I saw my father as too harsh and my mother as too weak. In my own experience as a parent, I have struggled with both extremes. I (Beverly) did not honor my father in the area of finances. He was a gambler and an intermittent good provider. In my experience, I have had great difficulty financially. At one point, I became very irresponsible, spending all my money and then had to ask my parents for money for groceries. The law requires this type of consequence.

We have used the terms "did not" and "were not able" to describe lack of honor. By "did not," we imply that there was overt choice to disregard parental wishes. By "were not able," we mean that even if there was a desire on the part of the child to honor a parent, that parent's behavior could not be honored. In the case of a child incested by a father, the child is not able to honor her father for that act. The parent's behavior requires a sinful response on the part of the child. This is a sobering, but true thought. Remember that a child can only respond to an offense in the context of the fallen nature he or she possesses.

We are often asked what it means to honor your parents. This question is most often asked in the context of anger. "How could I honor that *so and so* for deserting me when I was an infant?" We simply reply that the law requires us to honor the persons whom God has said are due that honor because of their position in the family. We need not honor what they have done, but we are required to honor them. To honor means to hold in high regard because of position. Thus, we honor the person holding the office of the President of the United States whether or not we agree with that person's policies.

However, God wants to do even more in our hearts. He wants to turn our hearts to our parents. More than passive honor, He wants an active love. The word of God declares, "Behold, I will send you Elijah the prophet before the coming of the great and dreadful day of the Lord: and he shall turn the heart of the fathers to the children, and the heart of the children to their fathers, lest I come and smite the earth with a curse" (Malachi 4:5-6, KJV). God knew that in these last days, the hearts of many would be turned away from their parents. This text identifies one of the special tasks of Elijah (God's last day church) as turning the hearts of parents to their children and the hearts of children to their parents. God wants us to experience His unconditional love for us so that through forgiveness we may be able to love unconditionally even those who so horribly wounded us.

The Law of Judging

The second basic law of the mind is that of judging. In Matthew 7:1-2 we read, "Do not judge so that you will not be judged. For in the way you judge, you will be judged; and by your standard of measure, it will be measured to you" (NASB). This is a positive command not to judge. However, do we not make judgments every day? Is not judging necessary in order to make correct choices of all kinds? The answer is yes, but that is not the kind of judging Jesus condemned as sinful. Judging another in the sense in which He means it here implies holding myself above another (the one I perceive as hurting me), judging his or her motives or intent, and doing so angrily. The bitterness associated with this type of judging eliminates forgiveness as an option and seeks revenge upon the one who hurts me. This Scripture predicts that how we judge another, that same judgment will come back on us. "What goes around, comes around," the popular saying goes. If we judge our parents as having abandoned us, then in some way we will also abandon others. It is true that our judgments may indeed be accurate; we may, in fact, have been abandoned. It is not that our judgments are accurate or inaccurate that makes them a problem. Bitterness in our hearts and judgment of the other's motive that make these judgments sinful and bind us to the consequences of this law.

We have seen this law play out repeatedly in the lives of those we work with. We will share several examples that will highlight this principle.

Ted was the oldest of three boys. His father was a womanizer and irresponsible with money. When Ted was thirteen and his younger brothers were ten and eight, his father left the home for good. Ted was very angry and bitter toward his father. Later in life, he married and had three sons as well. Ted had difficulties in the marriage and when his boys were thirteen, ten, and eight, he too walked out on his family. By the time we worked with him, he was seeking reconciliation with his family and could not understand his oldest son's anger. When we connected his childhood history with *his* father to what he did to his sons, he was shocked. The law is that specific. When you judge others in anger, bitterness, and resentment, you are doomed to repeat the behavior you hated the most.

Judy was born into a family where only one family member was not an alcoholic. Her mother was only fourteen years old when she was born. When Judy was six, her mother ran off with a man, leaving her in the care of her grandmother, who by this time had chosen to stop drinking. Judy started to drink heavily at age nine, and her drinking was out of control by the age of twelve. At sixteen, she had a son. She found an announcement about a revival at a nearby church while she was waiting for the liquor store to open. She began going to church and decided she wanted a better life for herself and her son. She came to us for counseling. Her dismay was palpable when we shared the law of judging as she discovered that she had done to her son the exact same thing that had happened to her: she abandoned him when he turned six years old! In fact, she did worse than her mother had done in that she abandoned her son, leaving him with strangers instead of a relative.

Patricia was a young African-American professional woman. When she was a child, her father had been unfaithful to her mother. Ultimately, he left her mother for a white woman. Not having resolved her issues with her father, Patricia married a man whom she helped through medical school. When he graduated, just as her father had done, he left her for a white woman. The law is always in operation. That is why it is a law. The Scriptures say, "Therefore you have no excuse, everyone of you who passes judgment, for in that which you judge another, thou condemn yourself; for you who judge practice the same things" (Romans 2:1, NASB). The specific result given in this Scripture is that we condemn ourselves to doing the very same thing that we hate the most in others. Do you remember saying that you hate such and such in your parent and that you will never do that when you grow up, and then find yourself doing the same thing? This phenomenon is a fulfillment of this law. God says that we are inexcusable when we judge. We look at the speck in another's eye and fail to see the beam in our own.

James 4:11-12 says,

> "Do not speak against one another, brethren. He who speaks against a brother, or judges his brother, speaks against the law and judges the law; but if you judge the law, you are not a doer of the law, but a judge of it. There is one Lawgiver and Judge, the One who is able

to save and to destroy; who are you who judge your neighbor?" (NASB)

We learn here that when we judge another, we not only judge the person, but judge the law also. We place ourselves above the law. Who among us believes that we can do this and not escape the judgment of the law coming back upon us?

One of our favorite sayings is, "If you spot it, you got it!" This reminder certainly keeps those of us who are in counseling positions humble. We have both seen the truth that we have done in practice, or in our hearts, everything that we help others to see in their own lives. The seeds of every evil are in each human being. None of us is better than another. Embracing our own depravity makes it easier to help others come out of their spiritual blindness. We share not from a position of superiority or self-righteousness, but from the vantage point of those who have intimately known those dark places of our hearts.

In many groups, there is a person who rubs another person the wrong way. When this occurs, we have come to recognize that there is often a judgment at work. We try to help the parties see how much they are like each other. They see their judgments in living color through the other person, and perhaps identify whom the other person represents to them. Often, issues are worked out through others who represent our father or mother. The Lord has a beautiful and humorous way of bringing just the right people to help us. One precious woman had issues with her 15-year-old son: his rebellion and her attempts to over-control. When she was in treatment, the Lord brought a 14-year-old client from another state who had identical issues as those of her son. Even though the woman's own son was not in therapy with her, she was able to work out many of her issues with him by the presence of this other young man. We had fun during those weeks when they were together. God kept these two tripping over their judgmental attitudes until they came to recognize them for what they were.

The Law of Vows

The third law we will discuss is the law of inner vows. Biblically, there were vows to the Lord that the person obligated himself to pay. The Nazarites took such vows (Numbers 6:2, Judges 13:5). The wise man says, "Do not be hasty in word or impulsive in thought to bring up a matter in the presence of God. For God is in heaven and you are on the earth; therefore let your words be few. When you make a vow to God, do not be late in paying it; He takes no delight in fools. Pay what you vow! It is better that you should not vow than that you should vow and not pay" (Ecclesiastes 5:2, 4-5, NASB).

The type of vow we refer to here is the inner vow. These vows may never be spoken, but are purposed in the heart and are, therefore, binding. What makes this type of vow sinful is that it is connected to the bitterness of our experience. Being angry about something that has happened to us and vowing that we never or always will do something binds us to what we vowed in one way or another. One woman came to us weighing approximately 400 pounds.

When she was a child, her father was an abusive alcoholic. She dealt with her pain even then by compulsive eating. The children at school began to make fun of her. Her mother, wishing to spare her daughter this humiliation, tried to control her eating, especially of her favorite food, ice cream. In her resentment against her mother's well-intended control, she vowed, "When I leave home, I'm going to eat ice cream until I get sick." This was her experience with ice cream every time until we prayed and asked the Lord to break the vow. Years later, she reported to us that she is still free from her compulsive need to eat ice cream.

Every one of us has made inner vows in bitterness at some time or other in our lives. Jesus wants to search our hearts (Psalms 139:24-25) and help us see our sin. Then when we sincerely come in repentance, He will gladly free us from the sin that has been binding us to its consequences.

The Law of Faith

The final law that we will discuss in this chapter is the law of faith. Jesus' experience with the two blind men illustrates this law: "As Jesus went on from there, two blind men followed Him, crying out, 'Have mercy on us, Son of David!' When He entered the house, the blind men came up to Him, and Jesus said to them, 'Do you believe that I am able to do this?' They said to him, 'Yes, Lord.' Then He touched their eyes, saying, 'It shall be done to you according to your faith'" (Matthew 9:27-29, NASB). In our experience, the law of faith indicates that our lives will go in the direction of what we believe. If I have been told that I am ugly, stupid, or a whore, and I believe these words, I will live out "ugly," "stupid" and "whoredom" in some way in my life. If I believe that I am not precious, I will seek out others to perpetuate this belief. They will not treat me preciously.

As victims (and we all are victims to some degree), we want to blame others for our problems. The law of faith, however, squarely places the responsibility (not blame) on our shoulders. Just because someone calls me a dog, it does not make me a dog. However, if I believe that I am a dog when they say so, I will start acting like a dog. Placing the responsibility on our own shoulders is good news. If the responsibility were another person's, then our freedom from bondage would depend upon the other person's change. If I, however, take the responsibility for my own choices, then I can repent of my sinful responses to life and be free. The best news is that we have a Savior who in fact took the responsibility for my life on Himself. He became sin and accepted my sin as if it were His own. His becoming the sin-bearer and living victoriously while carrying the weight of sin guarantees that, as I submit to Him, I too am, victorious and free.

Chapter 7

Forgiveness: Love in Action

> "Be ye kind one to another, tenderhearted, forgiving one another, even as God for Christ's sake hath forgiven you"
>
> *(Ephesians 4:32,* KJV*).*

The power behind God's command to forgive one another is that He has first forgiven us. The ultimate expression of God's forgiveness of us was the sacrifice of Christ on the cross. Christ's agape love expressed in His death is the seal of our forgiveness. His death empowers us to forgive those who have hurt us. As we enter into the death of Christ through our own personal crucifixion, we enter into the experience of His agape love. Forgiveness is inseparable from agape. We receive the capacity of Divine forgiveness when we receive Divine love. Agape is a gift, as the Scripture makes clear in Galatians 5:22: "[B]ut the fruit of the Spirit is love" (KJV), and Romans 5:5: "[B] ecause the love of God is shed abroad in our hearts by the Holy Ghost…" (KJV). In the same way, while forgiveness is a human decision it is more fully a Divine capacity received from God.

Forgiveness may be viewed as a decision regarding a debt. When I forgive, I decide that I am not going to collect a debt that you owe, because I owe a similar debt. We are familiar with this relationship between debtors as it is expressed in the Lord's Prayer: "Forgive us our debts as we forgive our debtors." I am not going to punish you even if the law warrants a punishment, because I require the same punishment. Forgiveness, however, does not mean only an absolution from guilt for me or for the one who has hurt me. The purpose of forgiveness is the restoration of communion between two parties. Ultimately, forgiveness is not just an act or a feeling; forgiveness marks the beginning of a new life, and in fact, forgiveness *effects* a new *way* of life.

This new way of life is purchased at a high cost to God, who forgives us; it is also costly for those of us who are willing to forgive others, because it involves self-sacrifice and a personal resurrection—resurrection to a life lived in Christ Jesus. True forgiveness causes my daily death, burial, and resurrection to a new way of life, which includes continual restoration and reconciliation to God and my human family.

As counselors, we are challenged when an individual says that he has already forgiven those who have hurt him, but his behavior indicates a lack of forgiveness. In essence, he is saying that he has the human capacity to forgive and that it is enough in his case. While it is true that we have a human capacity to forgive and that some have a greater innate capacity to forgive than others do. Advances in neuroscience helps to understand why. Your memory creates your future. That's because you imagine the future through the neural networks created by your past. It was true for the Hebrews, and it is true for you today. The experiences that will drive your responses in the future are embedded within your memory. No wonder, then, that we often struggle to release ourselves to God. We may have no template in our brains to facilitate that process. The way you understand and try to make sense of Jesus will be filtered through your memory and your story. That is because God generally works through the system that he created and called good, our mind/brain matrix. He uses our implicit and explicit memory functions, not only to draw us closer to him, but also to heal, renew, and vitalize those very functions. And this happens not only metaphorically.

For forgiveness to be established within you so that it flows as effortlessly as your breathing, you need to have some mental model of what forgiveness feels like in your memory. Otherwise, your life will feel dry as dust even if your theology is razor sharp. Despite what you assent to ideologically, you will still lose your patience. If forgiveness has not been modeled for you, it will also be quite difficult for you to anticipate a future in which you will readily forgive.[1]

Fortunately, God still pursues us and makes every effort to give opportunity to learn by experience what it means to forgive. Even though our human capacity to forgive may range from zero forgiveness ("I cannot forgive,") to maximum forgiveness ("I will give up my desire to punish or get even with you"), He provides opportunity to rewire our brains to experience the genuine article. The problem with our human capacity to forgive is that it is not pure, even in its best form.

The nature of agape love is revealed by comparing human forgiveness with divine forgiveness.

Human forgiveness is:

- Conditional: We forgive on the condition that the other person will change, and that we will not be hurt again.

- Changeable: If that other person does not meet our expectations, we put our forgiveness down and take up our resentment again.

- Self-seeking: We feel superior to the one we have forgiven and may feel justified in lording it over "that poor sinner!"

Divine forgiveness is:

- Unconditional: Our forgiveness is spontaneous, uncaused, and independent of the offending party's deserving it, or upon subsequent behavior.

- Changeless: Because it is independent of anything the other party says or does, it is complete and everlasting.

- Self-emptying: We enter into the other's experience and see how we are capable of doing the same thing or worse.

Matthew 18:21-35 is a beautiful illustration of these principles. With his human understanding of forgiveness, Peter asked, "Lord, how oft shall my brother sin against me, and I forgive him? Till seven times?" Humanly speaking, Peter thought that he was really extending himself. The scribes extended forgiveness three times, much as we commonly do. We have all heard or said ourselves, "Three strikes and you're out." Peter was offering perfect human forgiveness (The number seven signifies spiritual perfection). However, Jesus' answer challenged Peter's best human reasoning. The response Jesus gave, "until seventy times seven," was not meant to limit in any way the extent of our forgiveness but to convey to Peter and to us that even perfect human forgiveness is insufficient. The factors of seventy are seven and ten. Ten, one of the perfect numbers, signifies the Divine order of things. Therefore, seven times ten would signify perfect divine forgiveness, an order of things far superior to the best human forgiveness possible.

To drive His point home, Jesus told the parable of the king who took account of his servants. One servant owed him 10,000 talents, a talent being 750 ounces of silver. This number calculated to seven million five hundred thousand ounces of silver. The values of talents varied in Bible times, so it is not possible to calculate the exact value of ten thousand talents, but the estimate would probably be in excess of eight million dollars. The point Jesus was trying to make was that the servant could not possibly repay the amount owed. It is interesting to note that the servant thought that he could repay the money. Similarly, we try to do penance, make amends to God or "pay what we owe" for the sins we have committed. Knowing that repayment was not possible, the king forgave the debt. The servant then turned around and demanded that a fellow servant immediately pay him a hundred pence, which is about ten dollars. When the fellow servant could not, he had him thrown in prison. Jesus was attempting to compare the infinite pain and suffering that our sin cost God with the relatively minor hurts we inflict on one another.

We do not mean to minimize anyone's experience of pain and abuse. However, we want to state clearly that the worst pain a human being can suffer, including death, is small compared to God's redemptive sacrifice. The king was righteously angry with the one he had forgiven and delivered him to the tormentors, "till he should pay all that was due him." Because of our unwillingness to forgive others, how many of us have been delivered to the torment of consequence until we have paid all that we owe? We cause ourselves a lifetime of misery of bitterness, resentment, high blood pressure, and many more physical and emotional consequences. Jesus' words were plain: "So likewise shall my heavenly Father do also unto you, if ye from your *hearts* forgive not every one his brother their trespasses."

Forgiveness takes place in the heart. In the midst of the external ebb and flow of relationships, we can sometimes fool ourselves into believing that forgiveness has taken place. However, it is not until we enter into the death and resurrection of Christ that divine forgiveness will manifest itself in our lives and relationships. Jesus exhibited divine forgiveness as He hung dying on the cross. His thought was not for Himself, but for those whom He had loved through the ages, those who had crucified Him. His agape love was so total that His heart's cry was, "Father, forgive them; for they know not what they do." Though there was no malice in His heart toward those who were intent on killing him, their ignorance of *whom* they were killing did not erase their guilt. Jesus' forgiveness of them, essential to a manifestation of true agape love, did not remove the responsibility of Jesus' tormentors.

As counselors, we encounter three common misconceptions when we talk about divine, or agape forgiveness. The first is that many mistakenly understand that we are advocating that they continue to allow themselves to be violated and abused. The truth is that as Christians, we renounce all rights to ourselves, and eventually, we realize that nothing comes to us except as God permits. It is important to pause here and speak to what frequently happens with wounded ones. They unknowingly give away their rights to others. We are not advocating that. Before we can address this misconception, we position the wounded one to experience that in fact, God has indeed given rights to everyone. It is a choice to lay those rights down. There has to be a realization that one has rights before one can lay them down. Armed with this understanding, the wounded one can indeed choose to surrender to Jesus.

As long as we are Christians living on earth, we know that more abuse will come to us, as it came to Christ on earth. Along with our "rights" to ourselves, we also surrender our right to hold another accountable. Instead, the forgiving love of Christ seeks to find what is best for the other person. The best for the other person is something that only the Holy Spirit knows. As we go to Him for the answer, the Spirit will confirm in our hearts the best course of action. Forgiveness may mean separating for a time so that the other person can grow. It could mean setting a strong boundary, which includes separation with an offender who is not interested in changing, or it may mean staying in a very trying situation out of obedience to the Lord (1Peter 3:1-2). Divine forgiveness is so complete and perfect that what is best for the other will also prove to be best for me.

Geraldine was married to a man who was content to be a friend rather than a husband. Although she had known this for some time, Geraldine was surprised when her husband announced that he was not sure he wanted to stay in the marriage. This announcement came after twenty-five years of marriage, and immediately after the deal on their first house closed. Geraldine was hurt but she, too, was tired of the marriage in its present state. When she called us for prayer, she declared that she had a right to happiness with a real companion, not just a buddy. When we asked if she was willing to give up all of her rights and expectations of her husband and love him anyway, she adamantly refused. She was most vocal about her rights and questioned the benefit to her of giving up her rights. We challenged her to forgive her husband for hurting her, and invited her to experience the truth of the statement: "Forgiveness is so complete and perfect that what is best for the other will also be best for you." She wrestled with this thought for several days, and then called again to say that she had begun to pray for the willingness to give up her rights and for the ability to love her husband without expectations. Her husband's heart was softened when she approached him with this type of love.

The second misconception that arises from our bitterness at having been hurt is that if we do not hold the one who hurt us accountable, no one will. We are angry children walking around as adults playing a never-ending game of payback; in this game, there are no winners, and the cycle of "hurt people, hurt people" continues. As a young girl in Jamaica, Ruth was molested by her father. As we worked with her on forgiveness, she shouted, "How can you expect me to forgive such a man?" We asked her if holding on to her bitterness gave her peace in her heart. When she could see that her physical and emotional symptoms were the result of her insistence on carrying her bitterness, she was willing to let her bitterness go. In truth, when we try to hold others accountable so that they get what they deserve, we are playing God. He says in His Word, "Vengeance is mine; I will repay, saith the Lord" (Romans 12:19, KJV). God, in His wisdom, knows exactly how to hold our perpetrator accountable. He knows their history of woundedness as well as their sinfulness. However, God wants to hold the ultimate person accountable, and that is Satan. While we are busy trying to extract payment from the person who has hurt us, we are unable to look toward the future when all confessed sin will be placed on the head of him who is the ultimate perpetrator: Satan.

The third misconception is that forgiving means forgetting. There are those, especially in Christian circles, who say that unless a person forgets that something has happened, he has not truly forgiven. The question must be asked, does God forget our sin in the sense that He blots it out of His memory? Jeremiah 31:34 says: "[F]or I will forgive their iniquity, and I will remember their sin no more" (KJV). Likewise, Isaiah 43:25 states: "I, even I, am he that blotteth out thy transgressions for mine own sake, and will not remember thy sins" (KJV). Both texts use the word "will," not "can." When God says that He will not remember our sins, does it mean that He blinds Himself to our fallen human nature?

Although we have been justified and stand forgiven and complete in Christ, God has not had a spiritual lobotomy that prevents Him from remembering our sins or what has been done to us. The eternal nail marks on the hands of our precious Savior attest to the lasting effects of sin. Every time the universe sees the hands of His beloved Son, we are reminded of the enormous cost of sin. We will remember that forgiveness is not about absolution of sin alone, but about restoration of communion and reconciliation of brokenness. Our past should serve as a reminder of our glorious future.

What is it that God chooses to forget? He no longer counts sin against us. He has counted it against His Son. Since Jesus has paid the price, God will not remember to have us pay the price for our sin. It is in just this way that we are asked to "forget" the sins committed against us. Forgetting does not mean that we pretend that something did not happen. Rather, it means that we look squarely at what happened. We often say in counseling that the river of denial is different from the sea of forgetfulness. When a hurt comes, we choose to forgive because it is now a way of life for us. The power to change our heart toward the one who hurt us can come only from God. We make the choice to forgive. God cannot make the choice for us. However, once we have made that choice, He empowers us to forgive.

Neither does forgiveness mean that I will trust the one who hurt me. I can forgive, yet know that the other person is not safe. A woman who has been molested by her father would be unwise to allow him to babysit her children unless he has gotten help and done a great deal of work on his problem. Forgiveness is granted. Trust is earned.

If forgetting means pretending that something did not happen, we would ultimately be setting ourselves up for a pattern of repeated abuse. Too many of us are living in the river of denial. For years, I (David) was so verbally abused and emasculated that abuse seemed normal to me. I rarely fought back. When asked by others why I allowed this person to speak to me this way, my sincere reply was, "What way?" I was conditioned to believe that abuse was a normal way of life. I had long since stopped allowing myself to feel the pain of insults.

Forgiveness involves a process as outlined in the steps below. We want to emphasize that it is a process, which means that it is fluid. It also suggests that we may go from one step and then digress to to that same step again.

The **first step** on the journey of forgiveness is to embrace our story. Many of us in the river of denial do not know when we have been hurt. Many of us work hard to deny the pain we have experienced. We either consciously repress or unconsciously suppress the painful experiences of our lives. One of the first assignments we give our clients is to tell their story to a safe person or group. We also ask them to write it down because memories are triggered when a life story is written. There is often resistance to telling a story because of a fear of rejection. However, when the person experiences love and acceptance, great healing follows. Others are blessed by the sharing because everyone learns that they are not alone in their pain.

We are often confused about whether it is ok to feel the feelings related to our stories. The following is a helpful guideline for us: If a normal human being would feel hurt over what happened to us, then it is permissible for us to feel hurt too. Feelings are a normal part of the human experience and a normal part of the Divine experience as well. God feels hurt more deeply than we can imagine. It is what we do with the feelings that matter. Unsanctified hearts generate reactions of bitterness or, in emotionally repressed persons, denial.

The cleansing streams of forgiveness flow from the cross alone. Before we can fully forgive a hurt, we must choose to leave the comfort of the river of denial. This river is impure at its source, because while basking on its shores, we are concerned only with ourselves; indeed, we are blind to the things of God and others. The river of denial, therefore, is not entered without defilement. Once we leave the waters of denial and stand on the banks, naked before God, open to our real human feelings of pain, God takes us on a journey toward the sea of forgetfulness. This journey can be long or short, smooth or rough, as we require. The desert places of our hearts are often watered by tears held back for years. Wells in our bosoms that have long since gone dry because of the dams that we built for our own protection are filled to the brim with the release of overdue emotions. This is the **second step** on the journey of forgiveness: allowing ourselves to fully feel the pain of our abuse.

When we finally allow ourselves to experience our feelings, it may feel as if we are walking through the "valley of the shadow of death." However, we can know that our Shepherd is with us to guide and comfort us. The **third step** on the journey of forgiveness is allowing ourselves to experience the comfort of God. Without an experience of the comfort of God, it is nearly impossible to release the offender.

On our journey, we will be forced to see the thorny cacti of bitterness in our hearts. Although the needles of these cacti hurt everyone they touch, being willing to surrender our right to bitterness destroys them. Until this is accomplished, the sea of forgetfulness will remain a future hope, a daydreamer's fantasy. When the Shepherd sees that our openness to the Holy Spirit and we begin to experience our own brokenness and our need to be restored, He will lead us to the divine sea of forgetfulness and invite us to dive into it. In the sea of forgetfulness, we adopt a life that embodies the ability to forgive in our relations with others.

We must stay in this sea if we are to withstand the temptation to focus on self and maintain our place in the company of "forgiven forgivers" who join Christ in the ministry of reconciliation. Leaving the sea of forgetfulness through a refusal to forgive forces us to return to the valley of death, the desert of bitterness, or the river of denial. Because of the laws of honoring your father and mother, judging, and sowing and reaping, any who choose to leave the peace of the sea will be required to return, figuratively speaking, to the valley, desert, or river.

The **fourth step** on the journey of forgiveness is asking for the gift of being willing to forgive. Some have been so deeply hurt that they are stuck in bitterness. When we ask God for the ability to forgive, he is happy to change our hearts toward those who have hurt us. This power to forgive is a divine gift because it is not in our human nature to forgive—that is, to forgive because of agape, or divine, love.

We call the **fifth step** on the journey to forgiveness Gethsemane. Jesus, the spotless son of God, entered Gethsemane to become the Sin-bearer of the world. His humanity resisted the suffering of separation from his heavenly Father that being the Sin-bearer required. Three times, Jesus prayed to be released from drinking the cup of suffering, yet he resolved "yet not my will, but thine be done." After sweating great drops of blood, and making his final decision to redeem humanity, his new reality was that he became sin for us. I Corinthians 5:21 says, "For he hath made him to be sin for us, who knew no sin; that we might be made the righteousness of God in him" (KJV). Jesus' identity with us as sinners was so complete that He was made to be sin for us. His new identity with us as sinners allowed Him to suffer evil and to absorb it without passing it on. As the Sin-bearer, he willingly chose to suffer God's judgment upon himself and walked out of Gethsemane a changed Man-separated from his Father.

There is an application for us in our Gethsemane experience. We too must enter Gethsemane. As the offended ones, we are to identify with the ones who have hurt us. As Jesus sweat drops of blood, we too will to see how we are like those who have hurt us. We ask our clients to consider the following question, "How are you just like the one who has hurt you?" Often, clients resist this question because they cannot possibly see how they could be like their perpetrator. However, God wants us to see that if we were in the same circumstances, we would likely do the same thing. At the foot of the cross, we are all equal and stand in the same need. When resistance to this thought comes, we simply ask the client to ask God to show them how they are like their perpetrator. He always answers.

After we have surrendered in the realization that we are like our perpetrator, the second part of the Gethsemane experience needs to take place. We then pray in earnest to become the "sin-bearer" for our perpetrator. Our prayer will be something like this: "Lord, please roll the sin of my perpetrator upon me. I know to give it to you. I am willing to stand in the gap on their behalf. It is here at this point that we too, can stand up and walk out of the garden a changed person. We become separated from our right for revenge. Instead we get our justice from what Jesus has done. We become UNITED with the Father in his purpose to save our perpetrator.

There is a tendency to forgive self-righteously by looking down on the one who hurt us just as the Pharisee looked down on the publican. We pride ourselves in having mercy upon the poor, wretched sinner who has offended us. We are willing to forgive, but fail to see the pride in our position.

Although this prideful perversion of forgiveness may seem hard to overcome, we can look to the life of Jesus for beautiful direction. Before Jesus said "Father, forgive them…" on the cross, He first identified Himself fully with fallen humanity Thus, He broke the cycle of oppressed vs. oppressor, victim vs. victimizer. In the Garden of Gethsemane, Jesus made the decision to take on the sins of the world. Because of this decision, He earned the right to extend forgiveness to me in the name of my perpetrator. It has been a powerful experience when Jesus has said to a broken one, "I am so sorry that I have hurt you," when the true victimizer could not or would not. Only a Divine Victor could presume to extend such forgiveness on behalf on another, but when Jesus does, its healing effect is deep and lasting.

The judgment that should have fallen upon us fell upon Christ. As a result, not only did He experience separation from His Father, but He also felt the oppressive weight of temptation by Satan. Having irrevocably committed Himself to the task of redemption at Gethsemane, the only way out was to drink the cup. The other alternative, surrender to Satan, He would not choose. After He identified Himself with us and chose the pain of death for us, then only could He with meaning say, "Father, forgive them…" He had identified with us fully. *Because He did so*, and because He is the Son of God, His act also represents a demonstration of God's love for humanity. Therefore, Christ alone is able to minister mercy to the sinner; this role is demonstrated by His cry, "Father, forgive them for they know not what they do." There is no room for us to boast or to self-righteously forgive, because it is not ours to give. True forgiveness can come only from Christ. We are awed to receive what He has done for us, that we might be forgiven, break the cycle of rendering evil for evil, and minister mercy to others by forgiving them with His agape love, as He has done for us.

This sequence is necessary for a person's healing as well. To avoid self-righteousness, we must also identify ourselves with the ones who have hurt us. We must see the seeds of murder, rape, and molestation in ourselves. Paul's identification of himself as the chief of sinners was not mere rhetoric. He knew himself by experience. "For I know that in me (that is, in my flesh) dwelleth no good thing" (Romans 7:18, KJV). Often, bitter persons have been broken only when the Lord helped them to remember times that they themselves were the abusers. Even if we have not physically murdered, raped, or molested, we may stand guilty of these sins before the Lord because of the intent of our hearts. Matthew 5:28 says, "[W]hosoever looketh on a woman to lust after her hath committed adultery with her already in his heart" (KJV). If we were to see our hearts as clearly as God sees them, we would never put ourselves above another human being again.

After our experience in the sea of forgetfulness, when someone hurts us, we feel compassion for the other, we identify with him at some level, and we stay open to that person. We do not minimize or block the pain. Feeling the pain, and acknowledging our own guilt, we choose to forgive. Hence, the cycle stops with us, the forgiven forgiver. Instead of giving our enemies what they deserve, we give them what they need: self-sacrificing love. This act is the ultimate triumph over evil, for love goes where it has long been banished and shines in the darkest darkness.

The **sixth step** on the journey of forgiveness is making the decision to release the person from the debt they owe. Notice that this step is sixth, not first. Many Christians make the mistake of encouraging or requiring that a person forgive long before they are ready to do so. It is true that God would have us forgive as soon as possible because long-term bitterness destroys us, our relationships with people and with God as well. However, he understands that often it takes a person time to process the pain in order to make a decision to forgive. The time does not have to be long and the pain of the loss can be ongoing even after a decision to forgive. Think of the decision of Amish families whose children were killed to embrace the family of the killer immediately after the death of their children. This is an example of people who live in the river of forgiveness continually. Others who need more time to forgive should not be considered spiritually inferior. For some people, the decision to forgive must be made many times as they must live with the continual memory of loss of a loved one, the loss of arms or legs, or any loss that significantly impacts their lives forever.

The **seventh step** on the journey of forgiveness is prayer for those who have hurt us. Matthew 5:44-48 says,

> "...Love your enemies, bless them that curse you, do good to them that hate you, and pray for them which despitefully use you, and persecute you; that ye may be the children of your Father which is in heaven: for he maketh his sun to rise on the evil and on the good, and sendeth rain on the just and on the unjust. For if ye love them which love you, what reward have ye? Do not even the publicans the same? And if ye salute your brethren only, what do ye more than others? Do not even the publicans so? Be ye therefore perfect, even as your Father which is in heaven is perfect." (KJV)

In this familiar passage from the Sermon on the Mount, Jesus asks us to love and pray for our enemies. By making this request, which is actually a command, Jesus shows us that He desires to demonstrate the power of the Father's love through us. He invites us to come alongside our enemies in prayer to bring to their experience that which they do not have: love, compassion, and healing for their troubled hearts. Scripture says that it is more blessed to give than to receive. The greatest blessing comes when we serve our enemies. To serve them is to walk with them, take their "sins" as our own, and plead to God for them: "Father, forgive them, for they know not what they do." As Bonhoeffer says in *The Cost of Discipleship*, "We are doing vicariously for them, what they cannot do for themselves. Every insult they utter only serves to bind us more closely to God and them. Their persecution of us only serves to bring them nearer to reconciliation with God and to further the triumph of love."[2]

Our typical human response toward our enemies proceeds from a heart of bitterness. To be bitter is to be overcome by evil, and to return evil for evil. To be free of bitterness is to bless in return for evil, or to return good for evil: "Be not overcome of evil, but overcome evil with good" (Romans 12:21, KJV). Paul's statement is concise, but Peter's statement adds another thought: "Not returning evil for evil or reviling for reviling, but on the contrary blessing, knowing that you were called to this that you may inherit a blessing" (1 Peter 3:9, NKJV). We are specifically called to give bread and water to our enemies if they are in need: "If your enemy is hungry, give him bread to eat; And if he is thirsty, give him water to drink; For so you will heap coals of fire on his head, And the Lord will reward you" (Proverbs 25:21-22, KJV). Heaping coals of fire on our enemy's head means extending divine, loving forgiveness, even while we are being hurt. To paraphrase Bonhoeffer from, *The Cost of Discipleship,* The more bitter our enemy's offense, the greater his need of *forgiveness and* love (emphasis supplied).[1] Our reward is seeing our enemy changed and drawn to Jesus by our kindness. This attitude will be especially important in the times of trouble ahead. We will be persecuted severely, but our goal is to draw men to Christ through loving forgiveness.

How do we know that we have forgiven our enemies? Just as we cannot make a general confession of sin, we cannot make a general proclamation that we forgive everyone who has ever hurt us. As with sin, wounds occurred one at a time. Each hurt must be recalled specifically. The choice to forgive each hurt must be specifically verbalized in prayer. This specific choice opens the channel in our hearts to receive God's forgiveness: "For if ye forgive men their trespasses, your heavenly Father will also forgive you: but if ye forgive not men their trespasses, neither will your Father forgive your trespasses" (Matthew 6:14-15, KJV). Despite how we feel, we must trust that God has heard us and that He will give us the experience of that forgiveness. When we choose to forgive without feeling it, our prayer must be "Lord, I believe, help thou my unbelief."

Another guideline for determining whether we have forgiven from the heart is evaluating the present state of the relationship. If there is strain in a relationship that was once warm and open, there is more work to be done. It may mean that there is more pain to feel or bitterness to uncover. True forgiveness welcomes the offender into the warm embrace of an open heart of love. There are cases where to reunite with an offender would be dangerous to the victim and a temptation to the offender. In each case, God's wisdom will indicate how to apply these principles in a practical way. It is always true, however, that what is good for one party is also good for the other in such situations. The divine capacity to forgive, as an expression of agape love, will overcome the fear connected with such encounters. The willingness to embrace the offender will be present, even if it is not safe to do so.

The **eighth Step** on the journey of forgiveness is reconciliation. In God's program of forgiveness, it is not necessary to tell the offending party how much he/she has hurt us. However, God may at times indicate that such an interaction should occur. This step is not always necessary, because in Christian counseling forgiveness is an interaction primarily between a person and God, and not only between two human beings. When another human being hurts me, I go to God for comfort, and then I am open to His direction for what action to take with the other. Unless we understand this point clearly, many whose perpetrators have died would feel unable to "finish the work." However, God can do "exceeding abundantly" above all we can ask or think. If it is in my best interest (e.g., to overcome fear or shame), or in the other person's best interest, God will, make it clear that we need to speak with that person. The goal of such an encounter is not to just express feelings or "dump" on the one who hurt us, but to attempt a reconciliation. Matthew 5:23-24 states, "So if you are presenting a sacrifice at the altar in the Temple and you suddenly remember that someone has something against you, leave your sacrifice at the altar. God and be reconciled to that person. Then come and offer your sacrifice to God" (NLT). God has given us the task of reconciling people to him (2 Corinthians 5:18-20). We do this most powerfully when we attempt to reconcile with those who hurt us.

However, it is important to understand that not everyone is willing to be reconciled. In attempting reconciliation, we must respect the decision of the other, and not attempt to force them to reconcile. Our position is one of willingness to open our hearts to the one who hurt us. If the person refuses our overture of love, we can rest knowing that we have done what God has asked us to do.

The **ninth step** on the journey of forgiveness is boundary setting. Forgiveness does not require trust. Forgiveness is freely given, but trust is earned. Some people are simply toxic in how they do relationships. Others are not safe. If a father molests his daughter, she may forgive him, but if he has not gotten help to change, it would not be wise to allow him to babysit her children. Healthy boundaries must be established with people who have demonstrated over time that they are unwilling or unable to change. While God asks us to "turn the other cheek," he does not ask us to be codependent doormats for others to walk over. More will be said about boundaries in the final chapter.

In our discussion of forgiveness, the good news of what happened at the cross opens up a grander, loftier view of the heart of God. God, who is the perfect blend of justice and mercy, made us in His image. We too, have this sense of justice and mercy enthroned in our bosoms. When we are hurt as humans, we demand justice. This demand requires the shedding of blood, but not just anyone's blood, but the blood of our perpetrators. As Christians, we know that this is not right because God tells us "Vengeance is mine; I will repay, saith the Lord" (Romans 12:19, KJV). As we share our hurts with other Christians, we are reminded that mercy needs to be given to our perpetrators. However, we fear that our need for justice will go unsatisfied when Christian tell us to be merciful and forgive. However, God put within us a demand for justice that needs to be satisfied.

At the cross, Jesus demonstrated that justice can indeed be satisfied by offering up his blood. He can do so because he is the perfect victim, and because "He made Him who knew no sin to be sin on our behalf" (2 Cor. 5:21, NASB). Having taken the place of my perpetrator, He will come to me and ask for forgiveness as my perpetrator. In the conversation with Moses, God described Himself as I Am that I Am (Exodus 3:14). This description can only be complete when the "I Am" has a verb to complete who He is. He is whatever His children need. The dialogue will be "*I Am* sorry that I hurt you. *I Am* sorry for ... fill in the blank. He becomes willing to be crucified afresh at my hands by offering the hammer and the nail, willingly lying on the cross, and inviting me to nail Him to the cross as He takes the place of my perpetrator. As a victim, my need for justice is now satisfied. However, when I nail Jesus to the cross, I become a perpetrator. This requires mercy, which Jesus willingly offers, as He did so long ago at Calvary. When Jesus says to me, "Father, forgive him for he knows not what he does," He has satisfied in my bosom my need for mercy in one gracious act. I no longer have to look to my perpetrator for relief, but only to Jesus. The cycle has an end.

One additional gem related to Jesus standing in the place of the perpetrator can be found in the offering described in Leviticus 6: 1-7. Restitution is a vital part of the program God set up before a person would be free from the guilt of sin. In verse 5, the repentant one must "make restitution in full, and add one-fifth to it; he must give it to its owner when he is found guilty." In addition to repayment of what was lost, the offender had to ADD one fifth-twenty percent, a double tithe! Conviction, sorrow and confession are all desirable steps toward making peace, but they are not enough. They must be accompanied by a deep repentance that would make every effort to rectify the error and sin. This will in many cases include restoration, paying back with interest that which was stolen and making every effort to right wrongs. Because Jesus has taken on the sin of my perpetrator, he earned the right to restore that which was lost or taken from me. Now the promise in Joel 2: 25 makes sense.

> I will repay you for the years the locusts have eaten- the great locust and the young locust, the great locust and the locust swarm-my great arm that I sent among you. (NIV)

Within the confines of his law, Jesus is the ONE who will do the restoring, not only in the life to come, but in this life NOW! He is just and true in all of his ways! Praise His name.[2]

One final lofty glimpse is the application of the notion of God as the "first great cause." A good way to describe this is an analogy from parenthood. When our son Michael was a child, he was always running, jumping, and inevitably falling down and hurting himself. There is nothing like a mother's comfort, and as he ran crying to me (Beverly) for comfort, I would kiss the skinned knee and say, "Let me kiss it and make it better!" While I did not cause the injury to Michael, his pain moved me to say, "I'm so sorry that you were hurt." Our heavenly Parent does the same thing. While not responsible for the sin problem, our pain moves the heart of God. He *could have* but did not destroy Satan after his fall. Wounded ones often accuse God of being responsible for permitting Satan to live and wreak havoc upon humankind. He lovingly comes to us and says, "I am so sorry that you are hurt by this sin problem. *Not* destroying Satan after he sinned was the best thing to do. I am so sorry that you were caught up in this drama. I am ultimately in charge and take full responsibility for the ultimate triumphant outcome and everything in between. Although you may not see it now, please forgive me." What an awesome God we serve that He would humble Himself to us this way.

As counselors, we too have often apologized to wounded ones who have been deeply hurt. Although we did not cause the wound, we are willing to stand in the gap, to be the human voice to offer a needed apology. In this, we can represent God and be a tremendous source of comfort to these hurting ones.

This message of forgiveness has the potential to turn the world upside down. When we comprehend the cost of forgiveness to God, we can look to the future with anticipation to the ultimate triumph of God's love. Forgiveness is at the core of God's love. Indeed, it is the key to realizing His love in the lives of each of us, for all of us. His light lights the world and erases the darkness of hatred and evil— forever.

Chapter 8

Repentance for Sin: Cleansing Your Temple

> "For my thoughts are not your thoughts, neither are your ways my ways, saith the Lord. For as the heavens are higher than the earth, so are my ways higher than your ways, and my thoughts than your thoughts"
>
> *(Isaiah 55:8-9,* KJV*).*

God's solutions to our human problems are often rejected because they are incompatible with the carnal mind of man. We look for solutions that we can control, that are quick, and that allow us to continue doing the things we like to do. God's solutions, on the other hand, are radical. For example, the result of a second birth, or being "born again," is that we can have a completely new life! What could be more radical? The catch is that we have to give up sin, of course, and that is not always an easy process. In addition, we have to give up things we like to do if they prevent us from being happy in the new life God gives us.

The obstacle to these more radical divine goals is that today we live in a world full of people, including professionals, who take shortcuts to achieving success and happiness. For instance, God knows that it is not to our benefit to call sin "good," or to allow us to cater to unsanctified self in the name of freedom, independence, "self-actualization," or "free expression" of our feelings. However, in response to our psychological problems, many therapies have been developed. Most of these therapies are anything but radical, in the sense of the word used above, because they do not see a need for a radical change of heart, let alone talk about sin, and therefore allow us to continue our own unconverted, unsanctified ways. There is no absolute standard by which to track or measure a progression toward healing, which is based entirely upon the counselee's own feelings and self-perception of well-being. While respect for the person is of highest importance, it is our desire to facilitate a process that will result in the maximum blessing to the person. From a Christian perspective, this always involves a self-examination of the heart, and a genuine repentance for sin.

Jesus Himself is our model for healing.

> "And Jesus went about all the cities and villages, teaching in their synagogues, and preaching the gospel of the kingdom, and healing every sickness and every disease among the people. And when he had called unto him his twelve

disciples, he gave them power against unclean spirits, to cast them out, and to heal all manner of sickness and all manner of disease."

(Matthew 9:35-10:1, KJV)

Jesus Himself used divine power to heal the multitudes that came to Him, and then gave this power to His followers. God's Word is full of examples of Christians healing the sick. The question for us today is, "Is that same healing power available to us?" In the book *Desire of Ages*, Ellen White states:

> "'He that believeth on Me, the works that I do shall he do also.' The Savior was deeply anxious for His disciples to understand why His divinity was united to humanity. He came to the world to display the glory of God, that man might be uplifted by its restoring power. God was manifested in Him that He might be manifested in them. Jesus revealed no qualities, and exercised no powers, that men may not have through faith in Him."[1]

Christ's purpose for abiding in man and possessing his heart is not only so that we can find personal sanctification, but also so that He can bless the world through us. The following statement from Ellen White emphasizes this point from a different perspective:

> "When self ceases to wrestle for the supremacy and the heart is worked by the Holy Spirit, the soul lies perfectly passive, and then the image

of God is mirrored upon the heart. When the emptying of sin and the infilling of the Holy Spirit takes place in our hearts we may expect to see spectacular manifestations of God's power, not in fire, but in deliverance from sickness and disease."[2]

Here we see that submission (self ceasing to wrestle for supremacy) must precede the union of divinity with humanity. The result is that sin is emptied from the heart and the Holy Spirit fills us with His presence. God's amazing grace results in human manifestations of divine power to heal sickness and disease.

A biblically comprehensive healing ministry must address the every part of the human person. In this chapter, we will focus on healing of self-defeating thoughts. As 1 Thessalonians 5:23 says: "And the very God of peace sanctify you wholly; and I pray God your whole spirit and soul and body be preserved blameless unto the coming of our Lord Jesus Christ" (KJV). In the second chapter of this book, we discussed how the sanctuary service provides a ministry to the body, soul, and spirit. We will structure this chapter along the same lines as follows:

- Physical aspects of the treatment of the mind
- Conditions of the soul and their treatment
- Closing the door to demons
- Personal Sin
- Generational Sin

PHYSICAL ASPECTS OF THE TREATMENT OF THE MIND

The body and mind are continually influencing one another for better or for worse. Our body, soul, and spirit are not separate autonomous entities; what affects one will also affect the others. This is not a new concept. As early as 1910, physicians such as George M. Gould in *The Medical Review of Reviews* reported a link between a sweet diet and symptoms of ADHD. Largely, however, medical training has not emphasized the role of food related to mood and behavior. Barbara Reed Stitt reports:

> "In the sixties, when I was learning my profession, no one ever mentioned the idea that diet could have any bearing whatsoever on delinquent or antisocial behavior, except perhaps in instances of extreme starvation. We were told that every behavior had its roots in the social history of the subject. Likewise, psychiatrists learned that the cause lay in developmental deficiencies, and doctors were taught either to ignore such problems or prescribe a tranquilizer.
>
> "Yet the arrival of the late sixties and seventies heralded the birth of a tiny group of doctors, psychiatrists and others dealing with behavior problems who proposed a link between America's ubiquitous diet of processed foods and the enormous increases in crime, schizophrenia, hyperactivity, learning disabilities and a range of other emotional disorders which had hitherto been assume to exist in the mysterious realm of the mind."[3]

There has been a gradual shift to considering lifestyle factors such as diet, exercise, and sleep, as related to emotional and mental concerns.

We have worked with many depressed and even suicidal persons whose problems were largely related to diet. When they take in too much food, especially sweets, and damage their pancreas, they become hypoglycemic; as a result, they experience irritability and erratic changes in mood. They have not improved in spite of trips to psychiatrists and a course of antidepressant medications. An excellent book by Drs. Calvin and Agatha Thrash, *Nutrition for Vegetarians*[4], describes this syndrome beautifully and presents a dietary program for its treatment. We have used this approach successfully in many cases. When the dietary program has been adopted, there have been significant improvements in mood, and a lessening of irritability reported by the client and the family.

Rana was a woman depressed to the point of not being able to function. Rana could barely get out of bed to care for her children. Her estranged husband was threatening to take her to court to gain custody of the children. In addition to having issues of unresolved emotional pain, Rana's diet was filled with sugar and junk food. She was willing to do whatever it took to get well, including changing her diet. She steadily improved to the point that when she was taken to court, she was so strong that she won the custody of her children.

Excellent research has also been done on the relationship between other mental conditions and diet. Even conditions like schizophrenia are improved through dietary changes and nutritional supplementation. Abram Hoffer, M.D., Ph.D. has described his success in treating schizophrenia using a non-drug, nutritional supplement approach[5]. Those who are struggling with mental illness must be willing to stop smoking and drinking caffeinated beverages if they want to be successful in overcoming it. We have found repeatedly that individuals fall back into serious thought disorders when they do not eat a diet rich in the B-vitamins, and when they use caffeine and nicotine. These drugs leech the B vitamins, which are essential for brain function, out of the system. For the treatment of addictions, we recommend a non-stimulating vegetarian diet and a cessation of the use of all other stimulants, including nicotine and caffeine. We find that those who are willing to follow these recommendations are much more successful in their recovery. Not only is it well documented that nicotine and caffeine are powerful drugs that are injurious to health, but also they serve to medicate the feelings and, therefore, block a person's connection with God as well as his self-awareness. For these reasons, we recommend that everyone who comes for help stop the use of these substances when the counseling begins. We recommend natural remedies including herbs, steam baths, exercise, and trust in God to assist them with whatever withdrawal symptoms they may experience.

Weimar Institute, a renowned lifestyle center with an international clientele used the acronym NEW START to summarize the lifestyle issues essential for recovery of body and mind.[6]

- Nutrition in the form of whole grains and fresh fruit and vegetables
- Exercise that works the muscles and elevates the heart rate.
- Water that is pure
- Sunlight without overexposure
- Temperance (moderation in that which is healthy, abstaining from that which is unhealthy)
- Air that is pure and fresh
- Rest by getting eight hours each night
- Trust in God's will and provision

Those who bring their lives into harmony with these remedies will reap the reward of health for both body and mind. Following these principles of physical health makes it much easier for clients to deal with the deep heart wounds and the bondage of the mind.

A ten-day physical cleansing program—a combination of colon cleansing, fasting, juices, raw foods, cleansing herbs, and steam baths—prepares a person for the work of heart searching and cleansing that is required for overcoming difficulties of the mind. We have found the following principle to be consistently true: "As in the physical, so in the spiritual." Just as the body becomes overloaded with toxic waste when the laws of health are violated, so the heart can be filled with the toxic waste of bitterness and resentment from past wounds. Indeed, there are many relationships between the two worlds; for example, we can be both physically and spiritually blind, deaf, lame, and hard of heart. Simultaneously taking clients through a physical cleansing as well as a cleansing of the heart helps to highlight these parallels.

Conditions of the Soul and their Treatment

The soul is that union of body with spirit that results in our ability to think, reason, remember, and choose. The battlefield of the mind is where the controversy between Christ and Satan is being waged today. Therefore, we will begin our discussion of God's solution for the treatment of conditions of the soul with an overview of the topic of spiritual warfare, which is what we call the battle for the heart, the personal battle continually going on in the hearts and minds of all of us. Because of this battle, many of us choose to open the door to the enemy of souls. Others become his victims because of the actions of those responsible for them. Satan does not care how the door is opened. He will invade, possess, and oppress wherever he is given an opportunity. Spiritual warfare wins back to Christ that which Satan claims. It binds up and casts out the devil. It commands him by the authority of Jesus not to return. It teaches those who have experienced spiritual phenomena with demons how to resist the devil.

Closing the Door to Demons

Because we are on the very edge of eternity, the devil is working with "great wrath because he knoweth that he hath but a short time" (Revelation 12:12b, KJV). The special targets of the enemy's attack are God's chosen people.

He intends to undermine the work, and to destroy the workers. Christian children are being assailed as never before, but many parents are ignorant of how they open their children to demonic influences. Because children will play a special role in evangelizing the world, Satan wants to destroy as many of these potential soldiers as possible, especially the most gifted.

"Be well-balanced—temperate, sober-minded; be vigilant and cautious at all times, for that enemy of yours, the devil, roams around like a lion roaring, seeking someone to seize upon and devour" (1 Peter 5:8), Amp Bible). This Scripture is not meant to be a scare tactic, because we know whom we have believed and are convinced that He is able to keep that which has been committed to Him. "Greater is He that is in me than He that is in the world" (I John 4:4b, KJV). However, we must be sober and vigilant because the reality is that we are in a battle against a wily foe. To be victorious, we must become knowledgeable of his tactics and strategies. "To him that overcometh will I grant to sit with me in my throne, even as I overcame, and am set down with my Father in his throne" (Revelation 3:21, KJV).

From the beginning to the end of His ministry, Jesus was continually assailed by the devil. Not once did He fall for the devil's sophistry. He "was in all points tempted like as we are, yet without sin" (Hebrews 4:15b, KJV). Jesus' battles with Satan were fought for us. He could have stayed in the security of heaven, but chose freely to come to earth to win the victory that we had lost through Adam. It is important to understand that Satan has no power over us unless we give it to him as Adam did. In order to understand how to maintain victory, we will share several elements of spiritual warfare.

First, we must examine a concept that is essential to waging spiritual warfare successfully, that of legal right. When God created man, He gave him dominion over the earth (Genesis 1:26, KJV). Man was in submission to God's rule, or government. When man sinned, he rebelled against God's government, and Satan claimed legal right not only over man, but also over all creation on earth. Satan had the legal right to this claim since man had obeyed him instead of God. In the first chapter of Job, we see Satan exercising his legal right to represent the earth at a heavenly convocation of the sons of God (verses 6 and 7). Had he not sinned, Adam would have been at that heavenly convocation instead of Satan.

Satan continued to exercise this legal right until Christ's victory on the cross when "the accuser of our brethren" was cast down (Revelation 12:10, KJV). Christ said, "...now the ruler of this world will be cast out. And I, if I am lifted up from the earth will draw all people to myself. This He said, signifying by what death He would die" (John 12:31-33, KJV). Satan then began an intense work of persecution: "Now when the dragon saw that he had been cast to the earth, he persecuted the woman who gave birth to the male Child" (Revelation 12:13, KJV). Satan no longer has dominion over those who are Christ's who have been born again and do not walk after the flesh, but after the Spirit. However, He still claims legal right over any man who gives it to him, as Adam did. Many believe that Christians cannot be possessed by the devil, but we have worked with many sincere believers who have unconsciously opened the door to the enemy and have needed to have him bound up and cast out.

Listed below are some of the ways in which we give Satan legal right to possess or oppress us. It must be clearly stated that it is not only present involvement in these things that opens the door to Satan, but also any past involvement that has not been confessed as sin and renounced.

1. Involvement in games such as the Ouija Board, Magic Eight Ball, and certain computer or video games lets Satan know that we like his style of entertainment, and that we believe he will give us answers to our problems. Séances, palm reading, fortune telling, astrology, magic, ghosts, mental telepathy, and other similar practices are also directly spiritualistic.

Watching cartoons with spiritualistic themes, watching any animated program in which there are incantations, spells, or magic places our children on Satan's ground. In fact, Satan's deceptions often appear in a form that is "mixed" with morally acceptable or educational themes, especially in books or movies, but also in every form of entertainment. The entertainment industry is a primary target of Satan and his evil angels, because it influences so many of our children from infancy to youth, and into adulthood. These are areas in which addictions can be formed at an early age, but go entirely undetected unless parents are aware.

Our warning here also includes television shows with an occult or spiritualistic theme. In many of these media, Satan masquerades as a "good" or benign influence, even as a hero who wants to save the world. If you are involved in these activities and feel they are harmless, we urge you to place yourself on holy ground, and call upon Christ to strengthen your powers of discernment. Remember that in Revelation we are warned that Satan will appear as an angel of light, and even as Christ himself, an "antichrist" (See 1 John 2:18, 1 John 4:3, 2 John 1:7).

2. Addictive use of alcohol and other mood-altering drugs, but also any use of drugs in which the mental state is altered or weakened by chemicals, puts us in Satan's hands. All drugs are dangerous for this reason, but especially the hallucinogens. Tobacco and caffeine are also addictive and can weaken our resistance to the enemy.

3. Cult involvement characterized by placing oneself under the control of another man opens the door to Satan's influence. We must hasten to add that there are many sincerely deceived people in cults. Many of these people will find their way to the Lordship of Jesus Christ and to salvation. We condemn no sincere seeker, but know that God will lead all who are His to the fullness of truth. We must strongly state, however, that cultic involvement leads to demonic deception.

4. False religions, and related practices which are clearly pagan, have their roots in Satan worship. We believe that any religious practice that does not acknowledge the need for a savior does not lead to salvation. These spiritual practices are to be avoided.

5. False internal beliefs about self or others are lies that Satan loves to use against us. As the father of lies, Satan will keep us in bondage to himself by trying to convince us that we are lost, unlovable, stupid, or worthless. Many are deceived into believing that God has abandoned them, will not provide for them, or will not protect them.

6. Insistence upon, or even obsession with bitterness, resentment, hatred, or revenge places us right at Satan's door. These sins keep us from receiving God's forgiveness. (Matthew 6:14 says that if we forgive others, God will forgive us). These are the characteristics of Satan, never of God. Satan was the original murderer (John 8:44); these attitudes give him legal right over us.

7. Sexual sin is one of the most powerful means of control used by the enemy. When we indulge in personal sins such as adultery, pornography, or masturbation, and when we are victims of sexual sin through incest, rape, or molestation, Satan takes advantage of us.

8. Rebellion against or resistance to the God-given authority of parents, husbands, civil government, employers, or church leadership mirrors Satan's rebellion. The submission of the heart is one of the most important practices of Christian living that

we must learn in order to live victoriously in these last days.

9. Self-exaltation (pride) is a characteristic of Satan. Lucifer himself said, "I will ascend into heaven, I will exalt my throne above the stars of God…I will be like the most High" (Isaiah 14:13-14, KJV). The sin of Judas was thinking that he knew better than Christ how to carry out His mission.

10. Generational sin is passed on to us by grandparents and parents "to the third and fourth generation." Just as the predisposition to physical disease is inherited, a predisposition to certain sins may be inherited. Parental involvement in spiritualism and superstition, Satanism, or witchcraft may be passed on to children and grandchildren.

We are thankful that God has shown us a solution for release from the above obsessions, attitudes, and practices. We can free ourselves from Satan's control, and from his legal right to control us, by engaging in the following: 1) Specific heartfelt confession 2) Renunciation of the practices 3) Covering ourselves with the blood of Jesus 4) Death to self through the power of the cross and 5) Total consecration of the life to Christ and His service. We find that, when it is necessary, binding up demons and casting them out is best done by the person affected. The will of the person must be engaged to cast out that which he has invited in. We find this solution preferable to the approach where another person does the binding and casting out. The wounds that accompany sin can be healed only by the Divine Physician. This chapter has given an overview of the topic of spiritual warfare. Measures that are more specific must be taken with those who have been possessed, who have been Satanists, or who have been victims of Satanic Ritual Abuse. A discussion of these measures is beyond the scope of this book.

You may want to stop now and pray. Ask God how you may have opened doors for the enemy to come in to taunt and harass you. Some of you may have opened doors yourself. The actions of perpetrators may have also opened doors to the enemy. Take time to write down on a sheet of paper any openings that you can identify from each of the ten areas. Then take time to pray specifically with each list. A model prayer is given for each area of involvement. These prayers are designed to serve only as models, with specific points that need to be included.

1. Occult Involvements: Make a list of any occult activities you have been involved with. Prayer: Heavenly Father, I confess that I have participated in (Note to Layout: insert 3 lines). I ask your forgiveness, and I renounce (Note to Layout: insert 3 lines).

2. Alcohol and Drugs: Make a list of any alcoholic beverages and drugs you may have taken. Prayer: Heavenly Father, I confess that I have not treated my body as Your temple. I ask for your forgiveness. In the name of Jesus, I ask that You would give me the Mind of Your Son as a defense against the enemy of my soul.

3. Cult Involvement: Heavenly Father, I confess that I have participated in (Note to Layout: insert 3 lines).

I ask your forgiveness, and I renounce my involvement in (Note to Layout: insert 3 lines).

4. False Religions: The same format as 3.

5. False Internal Beliefs: Heavenly Father, I know that I cannot hold the breastplate of truth close to my bosom if I am clinging to any lies. I acknowledge that I have been deceived by the father of lies and I have deceived myself. I pray in the name of Jesus that you will rebuke any lying spirits. I see that I have believed many lies. I renounce the following lies: (Note to Layout: insert 3 lines). I choose to believe the truth as it is in Christ Jesus, my Savior. I lay my tendency to believe Satan's lies on the altar and ask that You bring it to death. Please plant the cross of Christ between this tendency and me. In Jesus' name, Amen. (False beliefs are discussed more fully in Chapter 9.)

6. Bitterness, Resentment, and Hatred: Dear Heavenly Father, I confess that I have not extended that same Divine forgiveness toward others that You have extended toward me. I pray that during this time of self-examination You would bring to mind those people I have not forgiven, so that I may do so. In the precious name of Jesus, Amen.

7. Sexual Sins: Dear Heavenly Father, You have told us to put on the Lord Jesus Christ and make no provision for the flesh in regard to its lust (Romans 13:14). I acknowledge that I have given in to fleshly lusts, which war against my soul (1 Peter 2:11). I thank You that in Christ my sins are forgiven, but I have transgressed Your holy law and have given the

enemy an opportunity to wage war in my members (Romans 6:12-13; James 4:1; 1 Peter 5:8). I come before You that I may be freed from the bondage of sin. I now ask You to reveal to my mind the ways that I have transgressed Your moral law and grieved Your Holy Spirit with any sexual alliance. (If you have been abused, molested, or raped, please include these individuals as well.) We suggest that you make a list of all persons with whom you have been sexually intimate outside of marriage. List those you have chosen as well as those who have abused you; then

a. Renounce and ask forgiveness for each sexual sin you have committed.

b. Renounce each use of your body by others: I ask in the name of Jesus Christ that the bonds formed by my union with these individuals be broken and that my body be rededicated as a pure and undefiled member of the body of Christ.

8. Rebellion: Dear Heavenly Father, You have said that rebellion is as the sin of witchcraft and insubordination is as iniquity and idolatry (1 Samuel 15:23). I know that in action and attitude I have sinned against You with a rebellious heart. I ask Your forgiveness for my rebellion and pray that by the shed blood of the Lord Jesus Christ all ground gained by evil spirits because of my rebelliousness would be cancelled. I pray that You will shed light on all my ways, that I may know the full extent of my rebelliousness. I now choose to adopt a submissive spirit and a servant's heart. Amen. The specific lines of

authority that are given in Scripture are listed below. Examine each area and ask God to forgive you for those times that you have not been submissive.

a. Civil government (Romans 13:1-5; 1 Timothy 2:1-3; 1 Peter 2:13-16)

b. Parents (Ephesians 6:1-3)

c. Husband (1 Peter 3:1-2)

d. Employer (1 Peter 2:18-21)

e. Church leaders (Hebrew 13:17)

9. Pride: Dear Heavenly Father, You have said that pride goes before destruction and an arrogant spirit before stumbling (Proverbs 16:18). I confess that I have not denied myself, taken up my cross daily, and followed You (Matthew 16:24). Because of this failure, I have given ground to the enemy in my life. I have believed that I could be successful and live victoriously by my own strength and resources. I now confess that I have sinned against You by placing my will before Yours, and by centering my life around myself instead of Jesus. I now renounce my self-life and by doing so, cancel all the ground gained in my members by the enemies of the Lord Jesus Christ. I pray that You will guide me so that I will do nothing from selfishness or empty conceit. I pray that with humility of mind I will regard others as more important than myself (Philippians 2:30). Through your agape love, enable me to serve others and in honor prefer others (Romans 12:10). I ask this in the name of Christ Jesus my Lord. Amen.

10. Generational Sin: Dear Heavenly Father, I come to You as Your child, purchased by the blood of the Lord Jesus Christ. You are the Lord of the universe and the Lord of my life. I now reject and disown all the sins of my ancestors. As one who has been delivered from the power of darkness and translated into the kingdom of God's dear Son, I cancel out all demonic working that has been passed on to me from my ancestors. By the authority that I have in Jesus Christ, I now command every familiar spirit and every enemy of the Lord Jesus Christ that is in or around me to leave my presence forever. I commit myself to You, Heavenly Father. I now ask You to fill me with Your Holy Spirit, to do His will from this day forward. I submit my body to You as an instrument of righteousness, a living sacrifice, that I may glorify You in my body. I commit myself to the renewing of my mind in order to prove that Your will is good, perfect, and acceptable. All this I do in the name of Jesus My Lord.

These thoughts have been adapted from an excellent book, *Steps to Freedom in Christ*[7], by Neil Anderson. It can be purchased at any Christian bookstore and it is highly recommended reading for these times. We can no longer hide from the reality that within our beloved Church are many who are suffering from their involvement with these sins.

Personal Sin

In the previous section, we have only briefly discussed several aspects of personal sin such as the choice to forgive or resent, to submit or rebel, and to be proud or humble. We have previously discussed that there are foundational laws that govern the health of the mind. The violation of these laws is sin. We read in 1 John 3:4 "sin is the transgression of the law" (KJV). God's solution to the sin problem in us is crucial to our understanding and victory. Unfortunately, in many circles today, even Christian ones, problems of the mind are not defined also as sin problems. They are defined as only psychological problems, or they are considered diseases that, by definition, we "catch." While there is some validity to defining emotional problems as diseases, this concept robs clients of the opportunity to take responsibility for their actions. Instead of minimizing our responsibility, squarely facing this reality allows us to get to the root causes of a problem rather than superficially treating its symptoms. Christian counseling should not teach formulas; it should encourage repentance and death to self, as we will see shortly.

The solution to personal sin begins with recognizing the problem. Jesus said that He came to give sight to the blind (Luke 4:18). He called the Pharisees "blind leaders of the blind. And if the blind lead the blind, both shall fall into the ditch" (Matthew 15:14, KJV). Lukewarm Laodiceans are called "blind," but they do not know their own blindness. They are counseled to anoint their eyes with eye salve that they may see (Revelation 3:17-18). Even as Christians, many of us have veils over our hearts and are blind (2 Corinthians 3:14 15). The veil is a metaphor for our blindness to the true condition of our hearts. The truth that in Christ the veil has been taken away must be received in our hearts. We are afraid of seeing ourselves as we are because we fear condemnation from others. We therefore condemn ourselves to spiritual blindness. Jesus wants to remove the veil and give us sight.

"The god of this world hath blinded the minds of them which believe not, lest the light of the glorious gospel of Christ, who is the image of God, should shine unto them" (2 Corinthians 4:4, kjv). Many "believers" have unbelieving hearts. The good news of the gospel has reached their conscious minds. They have made a mental assent to the truth, but their hearts do not trust Him. Hebrews 3:12 says, "Take heed, brethren, lest there be in any of you an evil heart of unbelief, in departing from the living God" (kjv). Even believers can be blinded when their hearts are unbelieving. One dear brother told us sadly one day, "When I hear you folks talk about John 3:16 and how God loves us, I just can't believe that it is true for me." His heart of unbelief condemned him to not being able to see in his heart the truth of God's love.

We need to see how we have responded sinfully to the events that have comprised our lives. Our natural human tendency is to minimize our responsibility, and choose not to see our sin. One of the greatest tasks of Christian counselors is to help their counselees see the full horror of their personal sinful responses to life. A person often makes an investment in staying blind, because when he sees, he becomes responsible for living up to what he sees. "If ye were blind, ye should have no sin: but now ye say, we see; therefore your sin remaineth" (John 9:41, kjv). The fight to bring sight to the spiritually blind, therefore, is a fight of love, a fight that may demand personal sacrifice. For this very reason, we have often said that it is easier to bring sight to those who are physically blind than to those who are spiritually blind.

When we have made the decision that we want to see ourselves as God sees us, we can begin to take responsibility for our actions. Our carnal nature prefers blindness to sight because we prefer self-justification and blaming rather than taking responsibility for our own actions. However, when we blame others or a "disease" for the way we are, we deprive ourselves of the possibility of taking advantage of the solution, which God offers. If I see myself as responsible for the problem, then the solution is also within the realm of my responsibility.

Many of our clients hold their parents accountable. They are so angry with their parents that they focus on their parents' sins and shortcomings rather than on their own. They blame their parents for the condition of their lives. We help them to see that they cannot control or change their parents no matter how much they may want to; they can only change themselves.

When I (Beverly) was five years old, we went for a family drive one Sunday. My father put me out of the car, left me under a bridge, and drove off around the block. As I looked at this event and all of the pain surrounding it, I began understanding the rage in my heart toward my father. I wanted to murder him and nothing short of that would satisfy me. When I was challenged with the choice to forgive, I asked, "Well, if I don't hold my father accountable, then who will?" The answer was simple: It is

God's job to hold our perpetrators accountable, no matter what they have done. It is not our job. God knows what we do not know. He knows their histories and wounds. He knows their hidden motives. "For the word of God… is a discerner of the thoughts and intents of the heart… and all things are naked and opened unto the eyes of him with whom we have to do" (Hebrews 4:12-13, KJV). He knows what to hold them accountable for. "Vengeance is mine; I will repay, saith the Lord" (Romans 12:19, KJV). Attempting to do God's job of judgment will invariably bring back upon us in some way the very thing we hate the most in the one who hurt us.

Once we have seen and taken responsibility for our sinful responses to our life events, we can have true heart sorrow for our sins. We have required the death of Jesus by our responses. We also have hurt ourselves and defiled many others with whom we have come into relationships (spouse, children, church family, and so forth). We must prayerfully examine ourselves, "Looking diligently lest (we) fail of the grace of God; lest any root of bitterness springing up trouble (us), and thereby many be defiled…" (Hebrews 12:15, KJV). We cannot have true heart sorrow for our sins if we have not been willing to release our parents from the talons of our bitter anger. Too often, we have seen individuals go through the motions of repentance and confession of personal sin and not experience the freedom from bondage which forgiveness brings. Because they have not dealt with their feelings about what happened to them, they are still harboring secret bitterness in their hearts. We also frequently see that individuals are motivated to stop the pain in their own lives, but have little regard for the impact of their sin on others. This type of sorrow is self-centered; it is not true godly sorrow.

True heart sorrow for sin leads to a thorough work of repentance in the life. "For godly sorrow worketh repentance to salvation not to be repented of" (2 Corinthians 7:10, KJV). Turning away from sin is something that we must purpose in our hearts to do. However, it is important to note that repentance such as this is beyond the reach of our own power to accomplish; it is a gift from Christ, who ascended up on high and has given gifts unto men. God gives us the ability to hate the sins we formerly loved. Further, He gives us a love for those who have deeply hurt us.

True repentance opens the way for confession. When we speak of confession, we are not talking about those personal sins that are between God and the sinner only. These sins need to be confessed to the Lord and to no one else. However, during the course of God's searching working to show us what is in our hearts toward others, the bitter roots that have been troubling us and defiling others are revealed. These sinful or fallen responses demonstrate a lack of honor toward parents, bitter root judgments, and inner vows. We have found it most beneficial for the individual to write out on a sheet of paper the fallen responses that he has made to life experiences. This is included in a process that we have entitled the Heart Examination.

Heart Examination

Directions: Ask the Lord to search your heart. (Psalm 139:23-24). Pray that He will reveal to you everything that He knows you need to see at this point in your recovery.

Events	Wounds	Fallen Responses	False Beliefs	Structures of Self
List the painful events in your life that you remember, especially from your childhood years. Also try to identify common patterns and themes in your home. Begin with one event or theme as you experienced it with a perpetrator. Finish the Heart Examination with that event/theme. Then go on to the next one. Be sure to do this assignment with all who raised you or those who had that responsibility. (biological parents, even if they left, grandparents if they raised you, etc.). Include any others who caused significant pain. Focus on those events which caused painful feelings such as fear confusion, or shame.	Focus on your feelings about the event or theme as best you can identify them. When you have difficulty getting in touch with your feelings, ask the Lord to help you. It is also helpful to imagine what the feelings of a normal child might have been going through your experience. Also, think back on us. (See Matt. 7:1-2 and Romans 2:1). Some of our judgments may be that our parents are controlling, weak, critical, unloving, abusive, etc. As the result of childhood pain, we make inner vows by which we are bound (I'll always or I'll never). These need to be identified and broken.	As unconverted children, we respond with a lack of honor toward our parents and bring a death orientation and a requirement that life not "go well" with us upon ourselves. (See Deuteronomy 5:16) In addition, we judge our parents and find that those judgments come	False beliefs are lies which we have believed in connection with painful life events. They are often connected to our sense of personal worth. If I was treated shamefully, I might conclude that I am of no value, essentially defective, will never amount to anything, am ugly, stupid and don't deserve to live. These lies keep us from embracing the truth of how God sees us and embraces us. Satan, as the father of lies, delights when he can deceive us this way. What do I believe about myself, other people, or groups of people (men, women), or about life in general?	A structure is a habitual pattern of responding to life which has been built into our character. These are the survival mechanisms by which we cope with the pain of life. A partial list of structures includes: - shame core - control/controlling - self-dependence - negativity - self-righteousness - judgmentalism - victim/victimizer - caretaking - noble martyr - family hero - perfectionism - self-sabotage - performance-oriented - fear of rejection - fear of abandonment - fight/flight - comfort through

We use the word "fallen" instead of "sinful" because so many of our counselees have been beaten with religion; in fact, the word "sin" triggers their shame to such a degree that they are unable to do the assignment. Carol, for example, came from a missionary family. Her parents were dedicated, but distant. She was verbally beaten with the threat of hellfire whenever she misbehaved. All of her life she was beaten with the word "sin." With individuals such as Carol, we must first work to heal their brokenness before we can help them to see their personal responses as sinful. Persons like Carol must begin their work in the Wounds column of the Heart Examination.

When we give the assignment, we ask that the individual pick one person to work on first. That person could be an offending father, mother, a stepparent, a spouse, or a non-related significant person. We ask him to make a specific list of his fallen responses related to that person. When he is ready, we often kneel together before the Lord and confess his fallen responses to Him. We are there to support the person as he goes before the Lord.

Often, those we work with have difficulty talking to God this way. They are unaccustomed to praying prayers of repentance and faith. They need someone whose faith can sustain them for a while. They sometimes forget things they want to present before the Lord. We often offer an opening prayer to help the person to feel comfortable. When the person is done, we pray a prayer of faith confirming in that person's mind that the Lord has heard him and that he has been pardoned. We declare by the authority of God's Word that he has been set free from the condemnation of the consequence that his lack of honor and judgments has required. We then ask him if he is willing to forgive the one who has hurt him.

At this point, we also ask him to tell the Lord that he has judged Him unjustly by imputing to Him the judgments that are really about his parents. Finally, based on Romans 8:1 "There is therefore now no condemnation to them which are in Christ Jesus, who walk not after the flesh, but after the Spirit" (KJV), we ask God to release him from any sense of self-condemnation for what he has done. Wounded ones are often the ones who have been hurt the most by the consequences of their sinful responses. They are very tough on themselves and beat themselves up worse than any of their perpetrators. Having condemned themselves to a life of bitter bondage and unwanted repetition of the very things they hated the most in those who hurt them, they carry deep guilt and shame. God wants to free us not only from the condemnation of eternal separation from Him, but also from the condemnation of punishing ourselves. We pray specific prayers asking for freedom from internal guilt and shame, and for internal peace.

When we have completed this process of forgiveness, we often see profound changes in those for whom we have prayed. They were freed from a literal bondage. Some experience a change in the way they feel. Others notice no immediate change but see the very real results of their repentance in their lives over the next few days or weeks. When the bitterness toward those who have hurt them is gone, their faces are much softer. They can converse easily about or with those who formerly created fear and anger. Essentially, they have experienced Jesus' forgiving righteousness, imputed not only in heaven, but imparted to their moment-by-moment relationship with Him. Forgiveness is no longer an abstraction, but a reality they have experienced.

Generational Sin

Work with generational patterns of sin is one of the most exciting and far-reaching areas of intervention that the Christian counselor is privileged to participate in. Not only is the individual's life freed from generational curses, but the whole family, and ultimately the whole church, benefits from prayer for the forgiveness of generational sin. Deuteronomy 5:9-10 gives the principle which describes generational sin: "For I the Lord thy God am a jealous God, visiting the iniquity of the fathers upon the children unto the third and fourth generation of them that hate me and showing mercy unto thousands of them that love me and keep my commandments" (KJV). In this commandment, God clearly specifies that what parents do affects their children and grandchildren. In addition, what our grandparents and parents did affects us today. This is a very sobering thought for those of us who have children. Given this principle, I know that the issues I have not dealt with are going to affect my children. Because of me, they will face the sinful patterns I have not overcome.

Normally, we do not discuss generational sin until after we have worked on personal sin, because our natural tendency is to blame past generations for our problems. Until the cycle of blame is broken, dealing with generational sin too soon might lead to the perpetuation of the cycle. Nonetheless, the power to change lives by dealing with generational sin and its effects is truly awesome. Many individuals have done everything they could to take responsibility for their personal sin. They have confessed and forsaken it, but destructive forces continue to wreak havoc in their lives. In these cases, the presence of a generational pattern of sin is likely.

One such case was that of a young mother, Pat, who had gone through the process of heart examination, repenting of everything that she was shown by the Lord. One morning we received a frantic call from Pat, whose nine-year-old son had been born out of wedlock before she became a Christian. She recounted that the previous night her son had violently begun raging at her to the point that she locked herself in the bathroom to avoid his abuse. She said that this was totally out of character for him, but that it was exactly what the boy's father frequently had done before they broke up. The curious thing about the situation was that her son had never known his father because he had left before the boy was born. We decided to treat this situation as a manifestation of generational sin. We prayed that the blood of Jesus would cleanse the bloodlines back to the origin of the generational rage. I spoke with Pat a week later. She said that after we had prayed together she had seen an immediate change in her son. The rage was gone. God's power does work to change the lives of those who do not even know that we are praying for them! It is important to consider three additional aspects of the principle of generational sin. The first is a genetic factor commonly reported in the scientific literature concerning diseases such as alcoholism, diabetes, and cancer. Years ago, Ellen White said, "The physical and mental condition of parents is perpetuated in their offspring. This is a matter that is not duly considered. Wherever the habits of the parents are contrary to physical law, the injury done to themselves will be repeated in future generations"[7]. Paul describes it this way, "Therefore as by the offense of one [Adam] judgment came upon all men to condemnation; even so by the righteousness of one [Jesus] the free gift came upon all men unto justification of life" (Romans 5:18, KJV). This principle applies in the physical as well as the spiritual realm.

Another aspect of generational sin is modeling or the example of parents. Children learn by what they experience more than by what they are told. Many adults model coping with feelings in a variety of negative ways. Among them are included: blaming others, raging, lying, avoiding, or medicating with alcohol, food, television, and a host of other analgesics. If parents model this type of behavior, children will likely mimic it. How many times have you said I will never act, parent or emote the way my parents have done? Despite your resolve, you find yourself reacting as they have done. By beholding, we become changed-changed into the image set before us. The learned factors in families contribute greatly to generationally sinful patterns.

The third factor in generational sin is the law of sowing and reaping. This law applies to generations and to individuals. Our children are going to reap what we have sown, "some thirtyfold, some sixty, and some an hundred" (Mark 4:20 KJV). Examples of this principle abound in

Scripture. Because of Abraham's sin with Hagar, Ishmael was robbed of his birthright as oldest son. Isaac had a similar experience when his oldest son, Esau, sold his birthright by Jacob. Jacob's plot to steal his father's blessing resulted in his having to leave home, depriving his father of his presence in his old age. Likewise, Jacob lost his own son, Joseph, and had to risk losing Benjamin in his old age. After this chain of consequences, we finally see the mercy of God intervening, but only after sincere repentance.

Children reap the consequences of their parents' sin. Sarah's suggestion that Abraham have a child by Hagar led to trouble for both Hagar and Ishmael. It also influenced Jacob having two wives against his will (Leah and Rachel). David's sin with Bathsheba not only resulted in the death of the child (2 Samuel 12:14) but also in sexual sin in his offspring (Amnon's sin against Tamar in 2 Samuel 13).

When we put all these factors together, we see not only that the human race is degenerating but that specific sinful tendencies are passed from generation to generation. Carl's story illustrates this reality well. His father was an alcoholic and a pimp. Carl's mother had been one of his father's prostitutes both before and after their marriage. Not only did Carl resent his father, but he was also furious at his mother for consenting to such a life. According to the laws of honor and judgment, however, he also became a pimp, and married one of his "ladies." His greatest pain, however, was that both of his daughters also became prostitutes who also married their pimps.

There is a need to diagnose generational sin, as opposed to personal sin (and often they go together). We first ask those we work with to identify their personal responsibility for the sinful patterns that are causing them problems. After doing this, we ask them to review their family history to discover any generational patterns of sin. These patterns can occur in any area of life, but are most often seen in the areas of addictions, sexual sin, finances, and spiritualism. Once these patterns have been identified, we then pray, asking that the blood of Jesus Christ, which cleanses us from all sin, be applied to the individual for whom we are praying. We also include all others in the family generations who are alive and who have been involved in the generational sin. We ask that the sinful patterns be crucified on the cross. Jesus always answers. He transforms these sinful patterns into family strengths. When spiritualism is identified as a part of the pattern, the powers of darkness are commanded to leave, with the permission of the one we are working with. We pray that God will surround the person with His presence to keep out the enemy.

The power of prayer for generational sin has truly astounding implications. The individual is blessed with freedom from the curse of the sin in his life, and so is the family. This happens even when the family does not know that the prayer is offered. This principle may be applied to the body of Christ, the church family. We can begin to see the power in Daniel's prayer (Daniel 9) and in similar prayers of intercession by Moses, David, and Nehemiah. The blind, lukewarm, Laodicean church of Revelation 3 is called upon to repent. What would happen if small groups throughout God's family would begin repenting and praying for the forgiveness not only of their own sin, but also for the forgiveness of the sins of their spiritual family in generations past and throughout the world today? We believe that there would be a revival and reformation in the church that would prepare it for Jesus' return.

Chapter 9

False Beliefs:
The Truth Will Make You Free

> It is better to live naked in the truth than clothed in fantasy (or denial).
>
> Brennan Manning

False beliefs are structures of self that are troublesome to most of us, but especially those who are wounded. False beliefs color our thoughts and feelings about ourselves and directly affect how we relate to others. These beliefs can be about ourselves, about others, or about the world around us. Jesus spoke about this in His healing of the blind men in Matthew 9:27-29:

> "And when Jesus departed thence, two blind men followed him, crying, and saying, Thou Son of David, have mercy on us. And when he was come into the house, the blind men came to him: and Jesus saith unto them, Believe ye

that I am able to do this? They said unto him, Yea, Lord. Then, touched he their eyes, saying, According to your faith be it unto you" (KJV).

The principle articulated by Jesus is that what happens to us in life will happen according to our faith or belief.

In those who have been abused verbally, emotionally, physically, or sexually, there develops a false belief system that can be described as a core of shame. This type of shame is not that sense of shame connected with the guilt of something that I have done. If I run a stoplight and get a ticket, a judge will ask how I plead. I reply, "Guilty, Your Honor." I am guilty of the offense, but the experience of getting a ticket and going to court also brings with it public shame connected to what I have done. This experience of shame (embarrassment) is normal and healthy, and the discomfort of it is a motivating force so that I will not break the law again. There is another type of shame, however, not connected with anything that I have done. There has been no violation of the law, and therefore, there is no guilt. This shame is not external, but internal, and describes a profound sense of worthlessness connected to my being. It is not about what I have done, but is about who I am. Shame-based individuals have a personal belief system that consists of messages such as, "I do not deserve to live." "I am worthless." "I am not loveable, important, nor precious." "My spouse, family, the world would be better off without me." "I deserve to be used and taken advantage of." "I am nothing." "I am less than others." "I do not deserve happiness."

Many who have been abused have asked us: "What do you mean by dying to myself? I already feel dead. You want to take the last shreds of self I have left." We state that they are correct. We want to take every shred of self and lay it before the Lord and ask Him to bring it to death. We have found in working with shame-based people that the miry clay of shame is mixed with the iron of pride, self righteousness, and judgmentalism. One part of these abused ones sees themselves as not enough. Another part of them, of which they are usually unaware, sees them as being more than enough. Their humility is a false humility that masks a deep core of pride. In fact, shame-based people are skilled controllers who manipulate their world in subtle ways such as passivity, procrastination, caretaking, and self-pity. Their controlling attempts are based in fear of their world falling apart if they are not in control. However, the evil of control is there just the same. Why is controlling evil? If I am in control of myself, then God cannot be in control. Controlling is a form of idolatry where I am putting myself in God's place.

In order to understand God's solution to the shame problem, we must understand the biblical view of our unsanctified self. The truth is that unsanctified self has been the problem since the fall of Adam. "Self," the carnal mind, "is enmity against God" (Romans 8:7, KJV). By nature, we are at war against God. Shame masks this war by giving a veneer of surrender and submission. Even while we are at war with God, seeking to displace Him from His rightful throne, He loves us and views us as precious. The tremendous contradiction is that while we are nothing of ourselves, we are also precious and of infinite value to God. A term we often use to describe this paradox is "precious worms."

Before we go into more detail about our value to God, let us look at Jesus' experience. Did Jesus feel shame? Was He touched with the feeling of our infirmity (Hebrews 4:15) in the area of shame? Jesus as the divine Son of God voluntarily chose to leave the security and peace of His heavenly home to come to a sin torn earth. He left His position as King of the Universe to assume the fallen condition of a man born after 4,000 years of earthly degeneration.

> "Let this mind be in you, which was also in Christ Jesus: who being in the form of God, thought it not robbery to be equal to God: But made himself of no reputation, and took upon him the form of a servant, and was made in the likeness of men: and being found in fashion as a man, he humbled himself, and became obedient unto death, even the death of the cross."
>
> (Philippians 2:5-8, KJV)

In Gethsemane, Jesus took on the sins of the world as if they were His own. He took on the experience of abuse the way other human beings experience abuse.

> "Priests and rulers forgot the dignity of their office, and abused the Son of God with foul epithets. They taunted Him with His parentage. They declared that His presumption in proclaiming Himself the Messiah made Him

deserving of the most ignominious death. The most dissolute men engaged in infamous abuse of the Saviour.[1]"

Indeed, Jesus knows the experience of abuse. He felt it more keenly than any other human being could because of His purity of character. Jesus had complete moral perfection; therefore, His capacity to feel was unlimited. He put up no wall or defense against feeling the effects of His abuse. He opened Himself wide to the experience so that He could relate to the multitude of abuses that all of His children would ever experience. If Jesus has borne our griefs and carried our sorrows, the question we must ask ourselves is, "Will I open myself to Him and allow Him to take my shame in whichever way it has manifested itself in my life?" It is best to ask as specifically as possible in prayer. As led by the Holy Spirit, identify any shame-based beliefs and feeling states. Pray about each, asking the Lord to remove it. Then believe that He has done what you have asked.

Some might respond at this point that God would never do such a powerful thing for them. However, the Lord longs for us to ask Him for what we need. He does not want His people to view themselves as worthless, because He sent Jesus who risked the possibility of eternal separation from His father for us. Therefore, He is pleased when we make the highest demands upon Him in order to glorify His name.

Will you believe that God's heart of love does not want you to carry this burden of shame? Will you have faith in His promise to take it from you?

Many of us have unknowingly played into the hands of Satan by believing the lies that He has sent our way. Often in abusive or neglectful families messages are conveyed verbally (e.g., "You are stupid" or "Shame on you") or behaviorally (e.g., playing favorites or making promises that are not kept). These result in a child believing that he is of little value. We must state emphatically at this point that it is not what was said or done that is the problem. Without condoning or justifying abuse (and this phenomenon seems very widespread at this point in the history of humanity), we cannot do anything about what was done. Even if we could, it is not our job to blame our parents, to judge them or to hold them accountable for what they did. That is God's job. "Vengeance is mine; I will repay, saith the Lord" (Romans 12:19, KJV). The root of our shame problem is that we *believed* what Mom and Dad told us. This is good news! It takes us squarely out of the passive realm of the victim and gives us the choice of whether to hold onto these self-destructive beliefs.

For many of us these negative beliefs operate at both the conscious and unconscious levels. They determine and drive all that we say and do. We are thoroughly shame-based to the core of our being. Satan, as a keen observer of human nature, uses these false beliefs against us to create discouragement and doubt. He has us right where he wants us. We have the choice about whether we will renounce and reject these lies. Satan is a liar and the father of lies (John 8:44). Our safety is in believing the truth, and the only authoritative source of truth is the word of God. In His word, God says that we are His children, precious to Him, held in the palm of His hand. Will you replace the lies that you have believed for the truth as it is in Jesus? At the end of this chapter, there is a biblically grounded list of affirmations with corresponding Scriptural support. This list is not exhaustive, but a good beginning for individuals who want to reprogram their brain to believe the truth. We would suggest that you take this affirmations list with scriptures (or create your own) and repeat the list to yourself at least once a day for thirty days. Do so prayerfully, asking the Lord to open your heart to receive the truths of His word. Also, make a list of the false beliefs or lies that you have believed. Aloud, renounce each lie. Tell Satan boldly that you will not believe his lies any longer. When he comes back to try to tempt you to believe his lies again, resist him with a "thus saith the Lord." As Christians we have the power of God available to us and the responsibility to "resist the devil, and he will flee from you" (James 4:7, NKJV). Satan cannot stand the pure truth. He must depart when we speak the word of God to him with authority borne of the truth of who we are to God.

In response to our prayer asking God to carry our shame, He in His wisdom may send into your life experiences and people to help you see whether you have completely surrendered your shame. Strong, overpowering people may come your way to see if you will wilt under their barrage. If your shame is gone, your response will be an equally strong yet submissive "thus saith the Lord." You will speak in *the authority of God, the truth of God*. Authority is the unfettered presence of God in the soul.

This is very different from how assertiveness is sometimes taught today. When I am assertive, I am asserting my rights and myself. Oswald Chambers states, "The essence of sin is my claim to my right to myself."[2] When I am speaking the word of God in the authority of God, I am out of the picture. "I am dead and my life is hidden with Christ in God" (Colossians 3:3, kjv). As Christ was both strong and submissive, so God's people can be. Other individuals may come into your life to hold you up, to be a support to you. We recommend that you find or form a Christ-centered support group. If you begin to be drawn back to your old patterns, others can help you to see it and support you in allowing God to complete the removal of any remaining roots. Although you have asked God to take your shame, it takes time to become rooted and grounded in the truth of the new creature that you have become.

> "That he would grant you, according to the riches of his glory, to be strengthened with might by his Spirit in the inner man; that Christ may dwell in your hearts by faith; that ye, being rooted and grounded in love, may be able to comprehend with all saints what is the breadth, and length, and depth, and height; and to know the love of Christ, which passeth knowledge, that ye might be filled with all the fullness of God."
>
> (Ephesians 3:16-19, kjv)

We praise God today that He has allowed us to go through the experience of shame to prepare us for the trials that lie ahead. As we allow Him to have our shame, and to experience His power, we will stand no matter how God permits in the future. We will not follow the crowd (yield to the popular demand) like we used to, but will stand for the truth to vindicate the character of the One we love. Find out from His word who you are to God and who He is to you. He will be your shelter in the time of storm.

Many find it helpful to reprogram their brain with the truths of the word of God. The old lies have grooved themselves into our brains. One way of forming new grooves is to repeat Bible truths daily for thirty days. The new belief becomes our new reality. For this reason, we have developed the following affirmations list based upon biblical truths. As you explore Scripture for yourself, expand the list to make it personal for you.

Affirmations List

Ways to Practice Affirmations:

1. Spoken silently to oneself

2. Said aloud to oneself

3. Spoken aloud to another person

4. Spoken into a recorder and played back

5. Written down on paper

Some Suggested Affirmations and Corresponding Bible Verses:

AFFIRMATION	BIBLE TEXT
I am a child of God.	Beloved, now are we the children of God. 1 John 3:2
I am precious to God.	Since thou was precious in my sight, thou hast been honorable, and I have loved thee. Isaiah 43:4
God Holds me in His hand.	Behold, I have graven thee upon the palms of my hands. Isaiah 49:16
I am beloved of God.	For God so loved the world that He gave His only begotten Son. John 3:16
I am not alone.	The angel of the Lord encampeth round about them that fear Him. Ps. 34:7
God wants good for me.	For I know the thoughts that I think toward you, saith the Lord, thoughts of peace and not of evil. Jer. 29:11
God will not abandon me.	Can a woman forget her suckling child, that she should not have compassion on the son of her womb? Yea, they may forget, yet will I not forget thee. Isa. 49:15
	I will never leave thee nor forsake thee. Heb. 13:5

Cleansing the Sanctuary of the Heart

Godls strength is available to me.	Fear thou not fo I am with thee; be not dismayed for I am thy God: I will strengthen thee; yea, I will help thee. Isa. 41: 10
In Christ, I am free to be me.	If the Son therefore shall make you free, ye shall be free indeed. John 8:36
In Christ, I set my sights high.	I can do all things through Christ which strengthens me. Phil. 4:13
I belong to God.	I have called thee by thy name; thou art mine. Isa. 43:1
I am special to God.	For he that toucheth you toucheth the apple of his eye. Zech. 2:8
God will give me good things.	The Lord will give me grace and glory: no good thing will He withhold from them that walk uprightly. Ps. 84:11
I am happy and at peace with God and with myself.	But the fruit of the Spirit is love, joy, peace…Gal 5:22
I will care for and accept my body.	Know ye not that your body is the temple of the Holy Ghost which is in you, and ye are not your own? For ye are bought with a price: therefore glorify God, in your body, and in your spirit, which are God's. 1 Cor. 6:19,20

I have a clear, sound mind.	Let this mind be in you which was also in Christ Jesus. Phil. 2:5 For God hath not given us a spirit of fear; but of power, and of love, and of a sound mind. 2 Tim. 1:7
I will always triumph over evil.	Now thanks be unto God, which always causeth us to triumph in Christ. 2 Cor. 2:14 But thanks be to God, which giveth us the victory through our Lord Jesus Christ. 1 Cor. 15:57
The strength of God is mine.	For the Lord JEHOVAH is my strength and my song. Isa. 12:2 Blessed is the man whose strength is in thee. They go from strength to strength. Ps. 84: 5,7
I will not be overwhelmed by fear.	When thou passest through the difficult waters, I will be with thee; and through the rivers, they shall not overflow thee. Isa. 43:2
I will not fear life.	Fear thou not for I am with thee; be not dismayed for I am thy God. Isa 41: 10 There is no fear in love; but perfect love casteth out fear. 1 John 4:18
I am free from the weight of sin.	If we confess our sins, He is faithful and just to forgive us our sins and to cleanse us from all unrighteousness. 1 John 1:9

I am safe and protected.	I will say of the Lord, He is my refuge and my fortress; my God; in Him I will trust. For He shall give His angels charge over thee to keep thee in all thy ways. Ps. 91: 2,11
I love doing my work, do it richly blessed.	Whatsoever thy hand findeth to do, do it with all they might. Eccl. 9:10
I am released from my past mistakes.	There is therefore now no condemnation to them which are in Christ Jesus. Rom 8:11
I have everything I need today.	Take therefore no thought for the morrow: for the morrow shall take thought for the things of itself. Matt. 6:34
The wisdom of God is available to me	If any man lack wisdom, Let him ask of God, who giveth to all men liberally and unbraideth not, and it shall be given him. James 1:5

Chapter 10

Death to Self: The Only Way to Life

> The last inward enemy of the believer
> to be destroyed is self.
> It dies hard;
> it will make any concession, if only
> allowed to live.
> Self will permit the believer to do
> anything,
> sacrifice anything, go anywhere, suffer
> anything,
> bear any crosses,
> afflict soul or body to any degree—
> anything, if only it can live.
>
> Poem entitled "Self Must Die"
> From gleanings of the late Esther Stein in the
> *Burning Bush*, 1951

This poem describes the struggle of death to self. We must die to every manifestation of self, and to self itself.

It is important to clarify these two aspects because this, in a practical way, is the gospel revealed in the life. Death to self is both the beginning and the end of the Christian life. It is the sign of true conversion and the evidence of sanctification. Consider the following:

> "Know ye not, that so many of us as were baptized into Jesus Christ were baptized into his death? Therefore we are buried with him by baptism into death: that like as Christ was raised up from the dead by the glory of the Father, even so we also should walk in newness of life. Knowing this, that our old man is crucified with him, that the body of sin might be destroyed, that henceforth we should not serve sin. For he that is dead (to self) is freed from sin. Now if we be dead with Christ, we believe that we shall also live with him."
>
> (Romans 6:2-4, 6-8, KJV)

These scriptures point out that our death is with Christ. He is not asking us to do anything that He has not done Himself. The promise is that after death comes resurrection. This promise is true for the spiritual death to self which baptism signifies. However, because too many Christians do not understand how self is manifested, they fail to not only overcome self, but also have not sacrificed self on the altar to God.

Baptism is an outward declaration of a complete surrender of the heart to Christ. However, too many of us have gone into the watery grave and come out the same as before baptism. Sometimes this is because of unwillingness. Other times, woundedness is a block to death of self. It matters not to Satan how he prevents the fullness of Christ's character from being manifested in the life.

We work with many who are willing to surrender to the Lord, but not completely. Frequently during a person's heart work, a crossroads is reached. The person must decide which way to go. One path is the narrow one: death to self, leading to spiritual life. The other is the broad path of living for self that leads to spiritual death. Most, with encouragement and support, choose spiritual life. However, it is not an easy choice, especially for wounded people. There is a present, living reality to the scripture: "Yea, though I walk through the valley of the shadow of death [to self], I will fear no evil: for thou art with me; thy rod and thy staff they comfort me" (Psalm 23:4, KJV). Wounded ones fear death to self. For many of them, it seems like the ultimate "evil." Their fear is that of total annihilation. They have struggled hard all of their lives just to survive, and now we are telling them that they must die to themselves. It is nearly impossible for some of them to grasp the idea. Some welcome the idea because they have had death wishes since they can remember, but they misunderstand the death of which we speak. Death to them would be the welcome embrace of oblivion. What we invite them to is new life in Christ Jesus. Many of them have been so hurt, even in the name of Jesus, that they do not trust Him. If Jesus becomes experientially real to these wounded ones as a healing presence, they will consider surrendering themselves to His control.

As part of the inheritance of the carnal nature, we all build structures of self into our lives to try to establish or maintain control. The roots of unholy control are always pride and/or fear. Structures are natural, habitual responses to life that we choose to build into our characters. We build these structures in order to shield ourselves from pain, not knowing that Jesus is our defense. Psychological terms for structures include coping, survival, or defense mechanisms. These structures help us to survive temporarily but can lead to bondage from which Jesus seeks to deliver us. "And deliver them who through fear of death [to self] were all their lifetime subject to bondage" (Hebrews 2:15, KJV). Structures are one form of modern idolatry, i.e., placing a practice or response pattern where God wants to dwell in our lives.

The building of structures of self happens in the following way. Because of our fallen human nature, we respond sinfully when hurt. This sinful response includes thoughts (judgments and vows), feelings and emotions (bitter rage, jealousy, and so forth), and sometimes actions (running and fighting). These thoughts, emotions, and actions are designed to keep us from being hurt again. These responses are often both automatic and unconscious because they occur without deliberation. We call these responses *reactions*.

To illustrate further, I, David, judged my father as too controlling. I felt angry about it and I ran away from home at the age of ten. At that point, my responses were personal sins resulting from my fallen human nature. However, I did not stop there in my evil responses. I continued to judge my father as controlling, not knowing how to forgive. As I continued to judge, judging others became a habit for me. I developed a structure of judgmentalism. The law of judging predicts that since my judgment was that my father was controlling, I too would become controlling. Since the law is invariably correct, I became too became controlling. Thus, I developed the structures of judgementalism and controlling behavior.

Not all structures are built to survive the pain of life. Many of them are simply rooted in our flesh, including pride, selfishness, and lust. Men and women manifest this sinful pattern when they make fashion and physical beauty idols in their lives. Men who subjugate their wives and children in order to boost their own ego have built structures that must be torn down.

We all must have these structures torn down—regardless of how or why they have been built. For wounded ones, the decision to allow God to bring these structures to death is hard. They serve as a hiding place from their attackers. Tearing them down means feeling totally exposed to abuse once again. However, we believe that the Lord understands that for a time in our lives, we needed to build these structures in order to survive. If we had not built them, we would be insane or dead. Nevertheless, the day comes in our walk with the Lord when He invites us to allow Him to tear down these structures. This means risking the vulnerability of openness to attack, trusting that He will be our protector as He promised. See Psalm 18.

There is no limit to the ingenuity of the human mind in building such structures of self. The following is a list of some common structures: (Note to layout: Insert Table 1).

Some of these structures are also forms of bondage and must be treated as so. Others, such as fear and depression, often need specific intervention besides bringing them to death. We have chosen two structures to examine more closely.

Performance Orientation

The need to perform is rooted in the inability to differentiate between being loved for who we are and loved for what we do. Love from parents is meant by God to be unconditional. However, as parents we often err by connecting our love with our child's performance. It is important for our children to know that we love them even when they make a mistake. When children are raised in a family where the only love they receive is connected to their performing a task well, it is natural for their sense of identity to be connected with performing well. Apart from performing, they are nothing. Doing well has been the only source of approval they have had.

Those who are performance oriented have great difficulty trusting anyone, even God. They are among the many professed Christians today who Hebrews 3:12 describes as unbelievers. They have made a profession of faith with their mouths, but have not believed in their hearts in a personal Savior who loves them enough to keep them safe. We are told in Hebrews 3:12 about believers with unbelieving hearts and that the result is a separation from God. Those with unbelieving hearts can never truly rest in God and in His promises to them. They do not trust God in the practical day-to-day experiences of life. "So we see that they could not enter in because of unbelief" (Hebrews 3:19, kjv). They have "received the spirit of bondage...to fear" (Romans 8:15, kjv) and "through fear of death [to self] were all their lifetime subject to bondage" (Hebrews 2:15, kjv). These Christians believe in the depths of their hearts that they need to be in control of their lives. They do not trust God or other people. They have learned to survive in life by organizing everything not only in their own lives but also in the lives of others. Their objective, which on the surface appears good, is to keep everyone happy, to keep the peace, but they pay a heavy price for this "peace." That price is the loss of their individuality, principles, and values. Their form of godliness is but a shadow. They are in a game of puppets and puppeteers alternating the roles of performing to please and controlling others with the strings tied to their past survival experiences. Such Christians may love the Lord deeply and are invested in doing many things to prove their love for God. In reality, they do not know the experience of God's love and are trying desperately to earn it.

When we believe that we have to be and can be good enough to earn God's approval, we are really practicing pagan idolatry: offering sacrifices to appease an angry God. We live a life of fear when we do not comprehend and receive God's unconditional, unearned loved. For many Christians, serving God and keeping high standards are nothing more than appeasement of an "angry

God." Never having experienced His love personally, we love Him the best we can, but unknown to us, our hearts are hardened in unbelief. Wounded ones have great difficulty comprehending the possibility of God's unconditional love. Because our hearts are hardened, we do not "hear His voice" (Hebrews 3:7, 8). We conclude, perhaps without even knowing it, that God has abandoned us or that He plays favorites and we are not one of the "chosen." The only option we can see is continuing to do what we have always done: run our own lives. How is it that we get to such a place in our lives? What leads us to conclude that we cannot trust God?

An important principle necessary to the understanding of this crippling phenomenon is found in Matthew 5:8. "Blessed are the pure in heart for they shall see God" (KJV). How we "see God" is formed largely in the early years of our lives. We will "see" our heavenly Father exactly how we have experienced our earthly father. We will impute to God the good or bad qualities we saw in our fathers. If our father was absent, broke promises, was harsh, could never be pleased, or was controlling, then our hearts will not be pure toward Him. There will be a lack of honor and judgments formed in our hearts toward God. We may judge Him as absent, untrustworthy, unloving, angry, harsh, judgmental, or critical. Although we may be very unaware of what we are doing, these bitter root judgments will reap a bitter harvest in our own lives. The judgments in our hearts are impure and make our hearts impure not only toward our earthly father but toward our

Heavenly Father. Therefore, we cannot see God as He is, but we see Him as we have judged our earthly father.

Pat was a woman in her fifties who was chemically dependent and had been in several fine treatment centers. She was feeling hopeless and depressed about recovery and felt separated from God. In exploring her history, Pat disclosed that her parents were both alcoholics when she was young and that her father had sexually abused her. We asked her to make a list of judgments she made toward her mother and father. We then asked Pat to substitute "God" for her father's name at the top of the list. It became clear to her how closely her judgments of her Heavenly Father paralleled those of her earthly father. She was willing to repent of her sinful judgments toward both God and her parents and to ask for the grace to forgive them. We then asked her to make a list of structures she had built into her life in response to having been hurt. She saw how she had become just like her father in the areas she hated the most in him. She asked the Lord to bring her to death in these areas. Since she prayed, she has been free to enjoy a trusting relationship with God.

For those of us who are parents, it is important to be aware of the things we do that connect our love for our children with their performance. We convey in many ways our conditional love for our children. We give attention only when the situation requires it. We affirm only when our children make the grades we want them to make. Since our expectations are so high, we may neglect the affirmation of our children when they have done well. Consequently, we convey the message that the child must do more to get our approval. They never quite measure up. For Joyce, whose parents were high achievers, it was expected that she get good grades. She received no affirmation for her high marks because she was only doing what was expected. No matter how hard she tried, it was not enough.

We express love only when our children obey. In a multitude of ways, verbally and behaviorally, we tell our children "I will love you if" rather than "I love you even if." Little Jason had a bad day at church, unable to sit still and be attentive. The message he received was "Mommy is disappointed that you did not sit quietly in church. Jesus is disappointed too." We do not condone misbehavior. However, how we correct our children will impact them positively or negatively. It is the first responsibility of parents to convey to their children their unconditional love. When we fail to do this, we are setting our children up to feel as if our love is based on their performance.

Use the following checklist to help diagnose performance orientation. Go through this list for yourself. Those that you check positively are indicators of performance orientation. You may question whether you have some of these symptoms. Often when we are reviewing this checklist with our clients, they do not see the full degree of their "performance." It then becomes necessary to illustrate from their own experience how some of these symptoms fit their lives. Many of us are blind and need spiritual sight. To some degree, we are all performance oriented, and therefore, must all ask that this trait in us be brought to death.

Performance Orientation Checklist

Please check those items that match your experience.

___ 1. Do you feel as if you need to be in control?

___ 2. Do you find it hard to admit it when you do wrong?

___ 3. Do you seek approval from others?

___ 4. Do you believe that you do not deserve the best?

___ 5. Do you have a hard time accepting it when someone calls you "precious"?

___ 6. Do you have difficulty accepting criticism?

___ 7. Are your expressions of love for others dependent upon their doing what you want them to do?

___ 8. Do you feel distress when others think badly of you?

___ 9. Do you make decisions based upon what others will think?

___ 10. Are you like a chameleon, changing to suit whomever you are with at the time?

___ 11. Do you feel like you have emotionally "prostituted" yourself to others?

___ 12. Do you believe that if you are not perfect, you are no good at all?

___ 13. Are you afraid of being out of control of your life?

___ 14. Do you have a hard time being spontaneous?

___ 15. Are you afraid of letting others get too close?

___ 16. Did you experience one or more of your parents as being rigid and controlling?

___ 17. Did you lack enough warm, loving attention as a child?

___ 18. Do you find it hard to trust others and yet find yourself trusting sometimes too easily and being hurt?

___ 19. Are you afraid to try new things?

___ 20. Do you sometimes do something "wild" or "crazy" just to see how others will react?

___ 21. Do you see being in control, especially in public, as being a virtue?

___ 22. Do you sometimes feel like you have no values or principles of your own?

___ 23. Do you sometimes feel as if you do not know who you really are?

___ 24. Do you always need to know the rules before you will try a new thing?

___ 25. Do you sometimes explode in a rage at someone "safe" and afterward feel intense shame?

___ 26. Do you strive for success and then sabotage yourself just before achieving it?

___ 27. Do you work for material goals, but still feel empty after you have achieved them?

___ 28. Do you sometimes feel that life is too hard and want to give up?

___ 29. Do you feel like a "noble martyr" when people compliment you for putting up with a difficult person or situation?

___ 30. Do you find it difficult to just relax or rest?

___ 31. Do you sometimes feel as if you are all alone in the world?

___ 32. Are you a person with "black" or "white" thinking (all or nothing)?

Victim Structure

Along with performance orientation, the victim structure is very common. A victim is a person who does not perceive himself as having a choice in life. Things "happen" to a victim. They feel powerless and expect that bad things are going to happen. As children of Adam, all of us are victims to some degree. We did not have a choice in being born with a fallen human nature. In our spirits, we cry, "Unfair! I did not ask to be born into this rotten world." "Poor me, something has been done to me and I'm not responsible for how bad my life has become." This sums up well the attitude of the victim. Blaming, another cardinal characteristic of a victim, began in Eden with Eve blaming the serpent and Adam blaming her and God. Most victims have been abused. The cardinal response, however, that makes one a "psychological victim" is the false belief that "This is what I deserve. Therefore, this is how my life is going to go. Why fight it?" The expectations that everything will go wrong and that they will be taken advantage of are the hallmarks of the victim.

Victims rarely fight for themselves in a healthy way. Abuse robs them of the internal strength to do so. They prefer wallowing in a pool of self-pity. Although victims find it hard to fight for themselves, they do fight. They are expert manipulators. They prefer an indirect assault to a frontal attack. Silence is often one of their most effective weapons. When backed into a corner, they can be fierce, unscrupulous combatants. Years of misplaced rage can gush out against one who has unwisely pushed the "victim" too far.

The victim cycle in families leads victims to become victimizers. The law of judging predicts that they will do the same thing they hated the most in their abusers (Romans 2:1). As victims, they become victimizers, and prey on others who are weaker than they are. Sometimes this victimization is conscious, other times unconscious. Victims who have become victimizers are horrified at what they do to themselves and others. "How can I be just like the one who abused me?" they wonder. Torn apart by their own guilt and shame, they beat themselves far worse than others ever abused them. Their abusers may stop tormenting them at some point. Victim/victimizers never stop tormenting themselves until they find peace in Jesus.

Below is a checklist to help identify characteristics of a victim. Please go through this list for yourself. Those that you check positively are indicators of the victim mentality.

Characteristics of the Victim

Check any of the following that apply to you:

___ 1. Do you have a sense of impending doom?

___ 2. Does it seem that bad things always happen to you?

___ 3. Do you tend to feel sorry for yourself?

___ 4. Do you tend to look on the negative side of life?

___ 5. Do you view the world as the "enemy"?

___ 6. Do you feel good when people compliment you about putting up with a difficult person or situation?

___ 7. Do you attract people who take advantage of you?

___ 8. Are you afraid that others will take advantage of you?

___ 9. Have you been in a relationship more than once with someone who was physically or emotionally abusive?

___ 10. When others raise their voices at you, do you wilt?

___ 11. Have you been "blind" to how others have used you? Do you make excuses for their behavior?

___ 12. Do you sometimes feel like a "doormat" for others?

___ 13. Do you have a false sense of loyalty to others, no matter what they've done?

___ 14. Do you feel inferior to others?

___ 15. Do you attempt to control others' lives out of a sense of fear?

___ 16. Do you let others dominate you in conversation?

___ 17. Do you have difficulty looking directly into someone's eyes during conversation?

___ 18. Have you been physically, sexually, or emotionally abused?

As stated earlier, many structures besides performance orientation and victim must be crucified. Ask the Lord to reveal your structures to you. The One who sees and knows our hearts (Hebrews 4:13) will surely help you see yourself.

"How do I die to these structures of self?" This is the question in the hearts of many Christians today. It is the Holy Spirit working in our hearts that helps us to see ourselves and what needs to die in us. It is the enemy's tactic to create self-contempt and self-condemnation, thus discouraging us. When the Holy Spirit shows us ourselves, it is never with condemnation, but conviction, and He then points us to the Savior. This is the eye salve that we are counseled to buy in Revelation 3:18. When we see ourselves as we really are, then we have a choice to stay the same or to allow God to change us. As we saw in the beginning of this chapter, death must come to both the manifestations of self and to self itself.

Begin with prayer, asking the Holy Spirit to reveal to you each structure that is keeping you from intimacy with God (Hebrews 4:12-13.). Make a list of the structures you own on a sheet of paper. Many times it is important to share this list with others in line with James 5:16. "Confess your faults one to another" (KJV). In my (David's) own experience, it was very important to be accountable to others in this process. I was so invested in looking good that I could not see many truths about myself. Thank God for those who loved and continue to love me enough to help me see myself. It is when we see, that we can really count the cost of the decision to die to ourselves. The next step is to admit that you have loved the "self" that you have built. In some ways, it has served you well. It has been a way of protecting self from external threats. God, in His wisdom, permitted these structures to remain unchallenged until He knew you were ready to live without them. It is an indication of God's confidence in your readiness that He has let you know that these structures are in the way of a greater blessing, allowing Him to be God in these areas now. Third, ask the Holy Spirit to help you see clearly why you built the structures originally. To let something go, one needs to understand the function it has served, e.g., survival, protection, peace. Fourth, tell the Holy Spirit that you are willing to hate that which you have loved. The Lord must change our hearts toward our structures because we cannot. Fifth, ask Him to bring about this change in your heart. Sixth, picture yourself at the foot of the cross with Jesus. Lay yourself out humbly before Him who died that you might live. Acknowledge to Him that you have been trying to live in your own strength without Him. Ask His forgiveness. Next, ask the Lord specifically to bring to death each defect and structure that you see. Eighth, believe that He has heard you. Finally, accept the resurrection life of Jesus (Romans 6:3-8).

We have found it helpful to kneel together to pray with a person who has made the decision to bring these manifestations of self to the altar. We do so in complete confidence that these structures will be crucified according to God's word. Paul said, "I am crucified with Christ: nevertheless I live; yet not I, but Christ liveth in me: and the life which I now live in the flesh I live by the faith of the Son of God, who loved me, and gave himself for me" (Galatians 2:20, KJV). This death is one of faith just as the life that we live afterward is one of faith. You may not feel different, but simply believe that God is faithful to what He promised. When your faith is weak, it is important that other Christians stand in the gap for you, praying words of faith on your behalf. Moreover, if words of faith are not enough, be assured that Jesus' faith is enough, "live by the faith of the Son of God." He already walked the road of death to self and came out victorious on resurrection morning.

Does this mean that we must make no effort on our own part to change? No! Faith is not magic. Character is built through a consistent, daily effort over the course of a lifetime. Most often, it is not built in the grand conflicts of life, but rather in the small, daily decisions to love that life requires. Make no mistake about it, the battle with self is the hardest battle we will ever fight as human beings, but because of the victory Jesus won, we are assured of victory also.

This death is one of faith in God's power and one of continual dependence on Christ. For these reasons, when we pray with our clients for their death to self, we pray strong prayers of faith. We ask that they be rooted and grounded in love for Christ and that their surrender will be not only of the structures which they have built (the manifestations of self), but a complete surrender of self. In this work, no compromise or reservation about your decision will work. All heaven rejoices in the decision of one of God's children to open their heart to a complete surrender to God's will.

It takes time to learn to walk in newness of life. Just as a toddler learns to take his first steps, you may feel unsure of yourself. Understand that you are not accustomed to walking in resurrection life. It is new and different. You will be tempted to return to the old familiar survival mechanisms you have used in the past. Satan will work very hard to undermine the new life of Christ in you. He hates Christ in you. Jesus allows these tests. They come to strengthen you, and to help confirm your desire for new life. They also challenge you to a deeper death daily. Remember Jesus' promise that no one could pluck one of His own out of His hand (John 10:28) and that Jesus began this work in you and He is committed to finishing it (Philippians 1:6). Rest in Him and let Him do it. He is more than strong enough.

Chapter 11

Boundaries in Scripture: Maintaining the Life within Us

> "Boundaries define us. They define what is me and what is not me. A boundary shows me where I end and someone else begins, leading me to a sense of ownership."
>
> Henry Cloud and John Townsend

The concept of boundaries is important to understand in experiencing cleansing of the sanctuary of the heart. People raised in stressful environments have poor, if any, boundaries. They come away from their childhood as living examples of Deuteronomy 5:9: "For I the Lord thy God am a jealous God, visiting the iniquity of the fathers upon the children unto the third and fourth generation of them that hate me" (KJV). Truly, the syndrome of the wounded person, often called codependency, is an intergenerational condition. It is passed from parents to children by active abuse (physical, sexual, emotional, verbal, social, and spiritual) or by passive abuse or neglect. Children thus abused or neglected grow into adulthood unaware of the truth of their preciousness and value in God's eyes. They have not experienced it in their interactions with those they have seen. Therefore, they find it nearly impossible to receive by faith the unconditional acceptance of the One who is unseen. Codependent persons, therefore, have poor boundaries. As the result of abuse or neglect, they will:

1. Gravitate to other abusive or neglectful relationships
2. Be unable to say "no" even to demands that are obviously abusive
3. Seek approval from their perpetrators to feel good about themselves
4. Carry the emotions of others

Recovery from codependency implies the development of the ability to establish healthy boundaries with oneself and with others in order to stop dysfunctional, self-destructive behaviors.

Many people believe that the concept of codependency is new, but while it is true that the term "codependency" is new, Eve was the first codependent. Even though God warned the pair in Eden in advance that the enemy would tempt them, with her tender heart, Eve was not able to discern the abusive intent of Satan. Deceived, she did not say "no." In offering the fruit to Adam, she tacitly sought his approval for what she had done. Adam became a victimizer to Eve when he blamed her for their sin. Satan victimized both Eve and Adam, in different ways.

After Eve had eaten of the fruit and brought it to Adam, he had a choice to make. He could obey God and not eat, trusting that the God who created Eve could give him another companion, or he could choose the relationship with Eve over his relationship with God. One can only imagine the struggle that went on within Adam as he pondered these alternatives. Those of us who have struggled with our relationships with others have a sense of Adam's conflict. Essentially, Eve became more important to him than God was; she became his god. How often has that been true for us! In Adam's case, there was no inherited weakness involved. His will was not weakened through sin. He talked directly with God, walking with Him in the Garden. He was warned about Satan. We see codependency issues, then, rooted in the sin of disobedience. The boundaries that had separated Adam and Eve from Satan were no longer in place. Fallen man became identified with the fallen angel. Satan's bent to sin now became humanity's.

After Adam's fall, every human being inherited his weakened fallen human nature. Jesus also, when He became man, took on our human nature (Hebrews 2). Jesus took our infirmities and bore our sicknesses (Matthew 8:17). He was tempted in every way, just as we are, yet He did not sin (Hebrews 4:15). Through His victory over His fallen nature, we too can be victorious over our inherited tendencies to put people or things in God's place in our lives. In fact, we must be victorious over them if we want to inherit the promise of eternal life.

Because of our fallen human nature, we do not know what is "normal." Our consciences have become so numbed and our wills so weakened that it is difficult to hear the voice of God speaking to us. Even when we become aware of our self-destructiveness or abuse toward others, we seem powerless to change.

How can we know with absolute confidence what "normal" is and how to behave in our relationships? How can we learn to hear the voice of God speaking to us and to follow His will? Our only sure source of truth is the word of God as revealed in the Bible. Our model of how to live is the Son of God, Jesus Christ. He is our hope of Salvation. He has sent us the Holy Spirit to be our constant companion here on earth. He ministers on our behalf in heaven.

God has written on tablets of stone His words (commandments, laws) which are our certain hope of safety if we follow them. God gave not to restrict our happiness, but to ensure it. "Thou through thy commandments hast made me wiser than my enemies: for they are ever with me. I have more understanding than all my teachers: for thy testimonies are my meditation" (Psalms 119:98-99, KJV). "The law of the Lord is perfect, converting the soul: the testimony of the Lord is sure, making wise the simple. The statutes of the Lord are right, rejoicing the heart: the commandment of the Lord is pure, enlightening the eyes" (Psalms 19:7-8, KJV).

God gave the children of Israel specific instructions to build an earthly sanctuary, modeled after the heavenly sanctuary, "that I may dwell among them" (Exodus 27:17-18, KJV). This sanctuary has an outer court surrounding it. This outer court is a boundary or source of protection for those within the sanctuary. The outer court represents Jesus and His law (the Ten Commandments). His commandments are a protection or a boundary to those who follow them. We can say with absolute assurance that those who study the Ten Commandments and have them written upon their hearts will abuse neither themselves nor others. God's word will be a lamp unto your feet and a light unto your path (Psalms 119:105).

The Bible contains specific instruction about how to establish healthy boundaries to keep unhealthy messages from affecting us. God created us as feeling persons. When a child feels pain, he cries; when he feels pleasure, he smiles. Feelings enrich our experiential lives here on earth, and will be a part of our experience for eternity. Who can imagine the inexpressible joy we will feel in God's presence for eternity? The other essential function of feelings is to warn us when there is something wrong. Physical pain and emotional pain are God's gifts to us telling us that there is a problem and they are an invitation to change. When, through abuse or neglect, we have poor boundaries, we are not only out of touch with our own feelings, but we carry the feelings of others—their shame, anger, pain, fear, and loneliness. When others overpower us by abuse, our God-given boundaries are torn down. An abuser is often working out his own unresolved feelings toward his perpetrators. The abuser's unresolved feelings are transferred to the recipients of the abuse (to the third and fourth generations). Reestablishing our boundaries involves experiencing our God-given anger, strength, power, and authority. What better way to do this than to go directly to the source of our strength, God Himself?

When a child is abused, God is angry. Jesus said "But if anyone causes one of these little ones who believe in me to sin, it would be better for him to have a large millstone hung around his neck and to be drowned in the depths of the sea" (Matthew 18:6, NIV). If God is angry when little ones are hurt, it is right for us to join Him in how He feels. When we see a child being abused, is not there an indignation that wells up within us that leads us to take action to intervene? If we feel a righteous anger about another child who is hurt, is it not okay for us to feel anger over our own abuse? It is righteous anger that enables us to set boundaries that say: "You may not hurt me any longer."

The concept of boundaries implies a place of safety, protection, strength, power, and limit setting. The Bible uses many terms to describe this concept.

> 2 Samuel 22:2, 3 says: "The Lord is my rock, and my fortress, and my deliverer; the God of my rock; in Him will I trust: He is my shield, and the horn of my salvation, my high tower, and my refuge, my savior; thou savest me from violence." Verses 31-34 and 36 continue: "As for God, His way is perfect; the Word of the Lord is tried: He is a buckler to all them that trust

in Him. For who is God, save the Lord? Who is a rock, save our God? God is my strength and power: and He maketh my way perfect. He maketh my feet like hinds' feet: and sitteth me upon the high places. Thou has given me the shield of thy salvation: and thy gentleness hast made me great" (KJV).

Notice the terms used: rock, fortress, deliverer, shield, horn, high tower, savior, buckler, strength, and power. God uses visual words to help us picture places and instruments of safety. The word "shield," for example, in the Hebrew also means "protector" and "defense" but also the scaly hide of the crocodile. The Hebrew word comes from a primary root word meaning, "to hedge about." What wonderful pictures for boundaries.

Not only are we protected in front but also behind. Isaiah 52:12 says: "[F]or the Lord will go before (in front of) you; and the God of Israel will be your rereward" (KJV). What is "rereward"? Webster's Revised Unabridged Dictionary defines "rereward" as "the rear guard of an army." God literally has your back.

Who is our protector, our boundary? Who is the rock under our feet, the shield in front of us, the rear guard behind us, the hedge all around us? It is God. He is our "strength and power." He is the source from which all power flows. Why use created objects to help us set boundaries when we can use the Creator Himself? Nothing can compare with God's protection.

Throughout history, God has shown His willingness and ability to protect those who ask Him, no matter how weak or timid the request. The book of Exodus records a powerful example of God's protection. God had done mighty works for the children of Israel to convince the Egyptian Pharaoh to release them from the bondage of slavery. When Pharaoh finally let them go, God protected them as a cloud by day and a pillar of fire by night. God stood before the people day and night to "lead them in the way" and "to give them light." However, this is not the end of the story.

Pharaoh began to regret letting the Israelites go, and pursued them with His whole army. Exodus 14:10 tells us that the children of Israel were terrified and that they cried out to the Lord. Was their cry one of faith? No, it was one of abject fear and denunciation of Moses and God. They said, "It had been better for us to serve the Egyptians, than that we should die in the wilderness" (Exodus 14:12, KJV). Moses counseled the people to be still and watch how God would deliver them that very day. God delivered Israel in a mighty way. Exodus 14:19-20 tells us first how God protected them. "And the angel of God, which went before the camp of Israel, removed and went behind them; and the pillar of the cloud went from before their face and stood behind them: and it came between the camp of the Egyptians and the camp of Israel; and it was a cloud of darkness to them, but it gave light by night to these: so that one came not near the other all night" (KJV). Psalm 105:39 says of this incident: "He spread a cloud for covering; a fire to give light in the night" (KJV). The Hebrew word for "covering" means a canopy, cover, chamber, closet, or defense. It is from the prime root word meaning to protect, encase, overlay, or to cover. God with His power protected the children of Israel from their enemies, even when they were very weak in faith and trust. He does the same for us today.

Can anyone honestly look at their life and not see the protecting hand of God, sometimes even before we had a relationship with Him? Isaiah establishes God's present protection for His people when he says, "The Lord will create upon every dwelling place of Mt. Zion, and upon her assemblies, a cloud of smoke by day, and shining of flaming fire by night: for above all the glory shall be a covering, and there shall be a tabernacle for a shadow in the daytime from the heat, from rain" (Isaiah 4:5, 6, KJV). How true it is that we have been in bondage to ourselves. God desires to lead us out of bondage, but many of us are more comfortable in our bondage. We do not trust God to protect us. Yet He has given us indisputable evidence of His desire to be our boundary. He is our protection through the wilderness of our recovery journey until we reach the promised land of perfect rest in Him.

Our study to this point has established 1) that the concept of boundaries exists in Scripture, 2) that the Bible contains many graphic illustrations for boundaries, 3) that God is our boundary, 4) that He has protected His people in the past, and 5) that He will protect His people even now. We will now examine specific feelings/emotions that tend to be carried or passed on from generation to generation and what the Lord says in His word that He will do to help.

Shame. Shame is one of the most devastating carried feelings. Carried shame occurs when a person, most often close to us, who has no boundaries, acts shamelessly toward us. Usually, shame is the byproduct of abuse. We come to believe that we are of little worth, deserving of this treatment, and feel inferior to others. Carried shame is emotionally self-destructive. It causes us to focus inward rather than outward and to get our affirmations from others outside of ourselves. Shame-based people react defensively to others. They have difficulty looking at others directly in the face and often hold their heads down. The Bible captures this condition beautifully and gives us a solution in Psalm 3:3. "Thou, O Lord, art a shield for me; my glory, and the lifter up of my head" (KJV). The Lord is our deliverer from shame. Again in Psalm 18:48, David writes, "He delivereth me from my enemies: yea, thou liftest me up above those that rise up against me: thou hast delivered me from the violent man" (KJV). What beautiful words of comfort for those who have felt "less than" as the result of violence done to us. God promises to lift us up not only to the level of, but above our enemies. What a great God we have!

Anger. When a person is subjected to abusive anger, he not only carries the shame of having experienced it, but also the anger itself. The combination of shame and anger results in rage. Most often, this rage is turned inward. Repressed anger is seen in symptoms of depression with occasional outbursts of rage. When we are carrying the burden of anger, God will lift this burden from us; He will give us His peace and rest, if we invite Him to do so.

Cleansing the Sanctuary of the Heart

He will be our boundary against those who do violence against us with their anger. As the Psalmist prayed: "Plead my cause, O Lord, with them that strive with me: fight against them that fight against me. Take hold of shield and buckler, and stand up for mine help. Draw out the spear, and stop the way against them that persecute me" (Psalm 35:1-3, KJV).

The Lord will teach us how to establish our boundaries against anger. Psalm 144:1 2 says, "Blessed be the Lord, my strength, which teacheth my hand to war, and my finger to fight: my goodness and my fortress; my high tower, and my deliverer; my shield and He in whom I trust" (KJV). For those who choose to trust in God, there is a promise of saving strength. "The Lord is my strength and my shield; my heart trusted in Him, and I am helped: therefore my heart greatly rejoiceth; and with my song will I praise Him. The Lord is their strength, and He is the saving strength of His anointed" (Psalm 28:8, KJV).

Many Christians are confused about anger. It is listed as one of the fruits of the flesh to be avoided in Galatians 5:20. On the other hand, we are told, "be angry and sin not" in Ephesians 4:26. When our boundaries are violated by violent behavior, righteous anger is necessary to rebuild them. If we see a child being abused, it is right, healthy, and normal to feel anger. In the same way, it is righteous to be angry over our own abuse as children. The difficulty is that our righteous anger has been repressed, or it is mixed in with a great deal of bitter, unrighteous anger too. In helping to sort out the difference between the two, let us look to the example of Jesus. He showed great anger and power when He cleansed the temple from those who defiled it. "And Jesus went into the temple of God, and cast out all them that sold and bought in the temple, and overthrew the tables of the money changers, and the seats of them that sold doves" (Matthew 21:12, KJV). Jesus' righteous anger was not self-centered. He was offended that His Father's house had been made a den of thieves. Anger that results in harm to another or to oneself is unacceptable to God. It is sin. Righteous anger is not sin. Rather, it empowers us to set limits and to tell others, "No, you may not continue hurting me." Spoken with love, but also with power, the victimizer know that he may not continue the abuse.

For those of us who have had difficulty experiencing righteous anger, our loving God is ready and willing to impart His strength and power to us, if we will ask:

> "Thine, O Lord, is the majesty: for all that is in the heaven and in the earth is thine; thine is the Kingdom, O Lord, and thou art exalted as head above all. Both riches and honor come of thee, and thou reignest over all; and in thine hand is power and might; and in thine hand it is to make great and to give strength unto all."
>
> (1 Chronicles 29:11, 12 KJV)

Fear. One of the most powerful and persuasive of all the carried emotions is fear. It is manifested in many dysfunctional ways in codependents including panic, phobia, controlling, reactive anger, withdrawal, and manipulation. Carried fear not only comes from abuse received at the hands of significant others, but it also comes from having basic needs neglected. We learn by experience that it is not safe to trust others with ourselves, so we learn to survive alone, "me against the world." For fear-based persons, relationships are shallow and unfulfilling. They may have developed a way of living that helped them survive until a crisis occurred.

As painful as these crises are, we believe that God uses them to show us our true condition and to draw us to Himself. Scripture is clear that God will be our boundary against fear, if we will permit Him to be. Psalm 56:11 states: "In God I have put my trust: I will not be afraid of what man can do to me" (KJV). This is a precious promise. All we must do is claim it in faith to make it our own. However, how similar we are to Christ's disciples. How weak is our faith.

The gospel of Mark tells us the story of Jesus and His disciples crossing the sea in a boat after a long day's work:

> "And there arose a great storm of wind, and the waves beat into the ship so that it was now full. And He was in the hinder part of the ship, asleep on a pillow: and they awoke Him and said unto Him, Master carest thou not that we perish? And He arose, and rebuked the wind, and said unto the sea, Peace, be still. And the wind ceased, and there was a great calm. And He said unto them, Why are ye so fearful? How is it that ye have no faith?"
>
> (Mark 4:37-40, KJV)

Satan was trying through nature to destroy the disciples, but Jesus showed them clearly who was in control. The disciples, however, did not understand or trust Jesus enough, before or after His death, to be without fear. They ran when the soldiers arrested Jesus. Peter denied Him three times. After His death, they were huddled in a room, afraid that they too would be killed for being followers of Jesus. How many of us have had similar experiences as we have struggled to trust God with our very lives? Making a decision to turn our will and our lives over to the care of God implies that we trust Him enough to surrender all to Him. To trust Him, we must come to know Him through prayer, meditation, and the study of His word.

What a contrast the disciples showed after they had received the Holy Spirit at Pentecost! They were fearless, speaking boldly and willing to suffer anything for the sake of Christ. They were now converted, and had surrendered their lives to Christ. His perfect love filled them. They were living examples of 1 John 4:18: "Perfect love casteth out fear" (KJV). Each of us has a choice to make. Will I choose to be converted, surrender all to Christ, and be filled with the strength of His love, or will I continue living the life of the fearful? This is a very personal, individual decision that only you can make. What will your decision be?

Loneliness. We all need closeness. To belong, to be accepted, and to be needed are among the most basic of human needs. In dysfunctional families, true intimacy is most often absent. The children take on survival roles (hero, scapegoat, mascot, lost child, etc.). Each of these is an attempt on the part of the child to be accepted and to get approval. However, with each of these roles comes loneliness and, at best, the illusion of intimacy. As these roles are carried into adolescence and adulthood, relationships become established with others outside our families using these same inadequate skills. The result is a continuation of the emptiness, which has always been present. Addictive behaviors are often attempts to fill the *void* we feel within.

Some people even turn to religion to feel better about themselves. Their attempts to relate to God are not based on a mutually intimate relationship. They do not know how to relate intimately. They attempt to relate to God, hoping that He will make them feel better. These people often need to step back and stop trying to "make something happen" with God so that they can surrender to Him and let Him lead. There is often great fear in this process. We are afraid that God will reject us. Nevertheless, God wants a truly free surrender, not a form of surrender. Because of childhood experiences, there is often a fear of abandonment at work. We fear being alone because we have been emotionally or physically abandoned so often. God has given us the assurance in His word that He will never leave us nor forsake us (Hebrews 13:5). The only way we can separate ourselves from the love of God is through our free, deliberate choice to do so.

God is *very* gentle and patient with us and constantly reassures us of His abiding presence. In Scripture, we are told, "Fear not for I am with thee, be not afraid, for I am thy God; I will strengthen thee, yea I will help thee, yea I will uphold thee with the right hand of my righteousness" (Isaiah 41:10, KJV). One of the most comforting metaphors used in Scripture to describe our relationship with God is that of sheep and shepherd. Isaiah 40:11 says, "He shall feed His flock like a shepherd: He shall gather the lambs in His arm, and carry them in His bosom and shall gently lead those who are with young" (KJV). Many of us are emotional lambs being carried by Jesus until we grow up to the point of following Him freely as adult sheep. Study this image in Scripture. It will be of great comfort. Jesus, before He left the earth, said: "I will not leave you comfortless. I will pray to the Father, and He shall give you another Comforter, that He may abide with you forever" (John 14:16-18, KJV). This Comforter, the Holy Spirit, is with us always. Jesus, Himself, is ministering on our behalf in the Most Holy Apartment of the sanctuary in heaven and will continue to do so until He comes again as He has promised. There is no need to fear being alone when the God of heaven seeks to be with us, to fill the *void*, the emptiness that each of us feels without Him. Our minds and hearts belong to Him, they are His temple, but He can only possess us as we permit Him to do so.

Jesus is our model. He is the way, the truth, and the life. He too was abused and misunderstood. He was different, set apart. His own people, the Jewish nation, and even some of His closest friends, rejected Him. Did Jesus feel all the real human feelings connected with rejection? Yes. Was Jesus' fear real in the garden of Gethsemane on the night before He died? Yes. Was His pain real when

Jesus hung upon the cross, carrying the weight of the burden of sin for the world? Yes! Was Jesus codependent? Did He have an unhealthy need to carry the world's burdens? We know that it is not possible for Jesus to have been codependent. What is the difference between what Jesus did and what codependents do?

The answer lies in motive and freedom of choice. Codependents give in order to get. They hope to get approval and feel better about themselves from giving. They do not have a choice except to carry anger, shame, fear, loneliness, or pain. It is a part of their addictive process. Jesus freely chose to give His life on the cross for us with no personal gain involved. He had nothing personal to gain but everything to lose in coming to this earth. His was not an impulsive decision based in a need to be loved, but had been determined from before the time of Adam's sin as the plan of salvation for humankind. God told the serpent (Satan) in Genesis 3:15: "I will put enmity between thee and the woman, and between thy seed and her seed (Jesus); it shall bruise thy head and thou shall bruise his heel" (KJV). The prophet Isaiah foretold Jesus mission hundreds of years before His birth.

> "He is despised and rejected of men; a man of sorrows and acquainted with grief...but He was wounded for our transgressions and bruised for our iniquities... and with His stripes we are healed. All we like sheep have gone astray; we have turned everyone to his own way, and the Lord hath laid on Him the iniquity of us all."
>
> (Isaiah 53:3-6 KJV)

Jesus not only carried the burden of our sins then, but He continues to carry our burdens now, if we allow Him to. He invites us: "Come unto me, all ye that labor and are heavy laden (grow tired or weary or are exhausted with burdens) and I will give you rest" (Matthew 11:28, kjv). What must we do to get this rest and refreshment of soul? Simply come and lay our burdens at the feet of Jesus. Psalms 55:22 says, "Cast thy burdens upon the Lord and He shall sustain thee; He shall never suffer the righteous to be moved" (kjv). He is our great burden-bearer and our boundary. He always has been, is now, and always will be.

References

Biblical Psychology

1. Cleansing the Sanctuary of the Heart: Hope in Our Wonderful High Priest

2. Joseph Luft, *Of Human Interaction* (Palo Alto, CA: National Press), 1969.

3. Curt Thompson, *Anatomy of the Soul* (Carol Stream, IL: Tyndale House Publishing), 2010, 6.

4. Daniel Siegel *The Developing Mind* (Florence KY: Guilford Press) 2012, 336-378.

5. Curt Thompson, *Anatomy of the Soul* (Carol Stream, IL: Tyndale House Publishing), 2010

6. Daniel Siegel *The Developing Mind* (Florence KY: Guilford Press) 2012, 336-378

7. Ibid 4

8. Alonzo T. Jones, *The General Conference Bulletin*, (Hagerstown, MD: Review and Herald Publishers), 1893, 404-405.

Healing Broken Hearts and Wounded Spirits: Opening Our Hearts to Jesus

1. For a fuller study of the issues of the concepts in the chapter, see John and Paula Sandford, *Healing the Wounded Spirit* (Bridge Publishing, 1985).

2. Diane Pappas, "Iron Deficiency Anemia," *Pediatrics in Review* 19 (1998) 321-322.

3. Bernie Siegel, *Love, Medicine and Miracles* (New York: Harper and Row, 1986).

4. Gerald May, *Care of Mind/Care of Spirit* (New York: Harper Collins, 1992).

5. For a fuller description of addiction in the chapter, see Gerald May, *Addiction and Grace* (Harper Collins Publishing, 1988)

6. Ibid 11

7. Vincent J. Felitti, et. al., Relationship of Childhood Abuse and Household Dysfunction to Many of the Leading Causes of Death in Adults: The Adverse Childhood Experiences (ACE) Study," *American Journal of Preventive Medicine* 14:4,(1998): 245-258. Also, Adverse Childhood Experiences (ACE) Study, Division of Adult and Community Health, National Center for Chronic Disease Prevention and Health Promotion.

8. Curt Thompson, *Anatomy of the Soul* (Carol Stream, IL: Tyndale House Publishing 2010).

9. Miller, Greg Learning to Forget. By:, *Science*, 304:4, (2004):34-36. Issue 5667.

10. Ellen G. White, *Desire of Ages* (Hagerstown, MD: Review and Herald Publishing, 1898), 710.

11. Ibid. 483.

The Law of Love: God's Antidote for Sin

1. Ellen G. White, *Patriarchs and Prophets* (Hagerstown, MD: Review and Herald, 1890) 34-35.

2. Ellen G. White, *Desire of Ages* (Hagerstown, Md: Review and Herald,1898) 20-21.

The Height and Depth of Law: What Was Natural became Unnatural

1. The basis for many of the concepts relating to the therapeutic role of the law we owe to John and Paula Sandford. Their book *Transformation of the Inner Man*, Bridge Publishing, 1982, contains a more detailed discussion of this subject.

The Laws of Honor, Judging, Vows, and Faith: God's Accommodation for Sin Forgiveness: Love in Action

1. Curt Thompson, *The Anatomy of the Soul* (Carol Stream, IL: Tyndale House Publishing 2010) 83

2. Dietrich Bonhoeffer, *The Cost of Discipleship* (New York: Touchstone, 1959), 149.

Repentance for Sin: Cleansing Your Temple

1. Ellen G. White, *Desire of Ages* (Hagerstown, MD: Review and Herald Publishers, 1898) 664.

2. Ellen G. White, "Manuscript 176," in *Manuscript Releases* (Hagerstown, MD: Review and Herald Publishing, 1898).

3. Barbara Reed Stitt, *Food and Behavior* (Kenosha, WI: Natural Press, 1997), 20-21.

4. Calvin Thrash and Agatha Thrash, *Nutrition for Vegetarians* (Seele, AL: Uchee Pines 1982).

5. Abram Hoffer, "Treatment of Schizophrenia," *Orthomolecular Psychiatry*, 3:4 (1974), 280-290.

6. www.newstart.com/what_is.php

7. Neil T. Anderson, *The Steps to Freedom in Christ* (Ventura, CA: Regal Books, 2004).

False Beliefs: The Truth will Make You Free

1. Ellen G. White, *Desire of Ages* (Hagerstown, MD: Review and Herald Publishing,1898), 715.

2. Oswald Chambers, *The Complete Works of Oswald Chambers*, (Grand Rapids, MI: Discovery House Publishers, 2000), 234.

Death to Self: The Only Way to Life Boundaries in Scripture: Maintaining the Life within Us

1. For more information on this subject, we refer you to a classic on the subject: Cloud, Henry and John Townsend *Boundaries: When to Say Yes, When to Say No-To Take Control of Your Life* (Grand Rapids, MI: Zondevan) 1992